escapes!

• • •

true stories from the edge

true stories from the edge

Laura Scandiffio

escapes!

ANNICK PRESS

TORONTO + NEW YORK + VANCOUVER

Annick Press Ltd.

All rights reserved. No part of this work covered by the copyrights hereon may be reproduced or used in any form or by any means — graphic, electronic, or mechanical — without the prior written permission of the publisher.

We acknowledge the support of the Canada Council for the Arts, the Ontario Arts Council, the Government of Ontario through the Ontario Book Publishers Tax Credit program and the Ontario Book Initiative, and the Government of Canada through the Book Publishing Industry Development Program (BPIDP) for our publishing activities.

Edited by Pam Robertson
Copy edited by Pam Robertson
Cover art by Scott Cameron
Design by Irvin Cheung/iCheung Design

Cataloging in Publication Data

Scandiffio, Laura

    Escapes! / written by Laura Scandiffio ; illustrated by Stephen MacEachern.

(True stories from the edge)
Includes index.
ISBN 1-55037-823-6 (bound).—ISBN 1-55037-822-8 (pbk.)

    1. Escapes—Juvenile literature. I. MacEachern, Stephen II. Title. III. Series.

G525.S23 2003   j904   C2003-901897-0

The text was typeset in Bembo.

Distributed in Canada by	Distributed in the U.S.A. by	Published in the U.S.A. by
Firefly Books Ltd.	Firefly Books (U.S.) Inc.	Annick Press (U.S.) Ltd.
3680 Victoria Park Avenue	P.O. Box 1338	
Willowdale, ON	Ellicott Station	
M2H 3K1	Buffalo, NY 14205	

Printed and bound in Canada by Friesens, Altona, Manitoba

Visit us at **www.annickpress.com**

Contents

Introduction
Struggles for Freedom

A SLAVE, CHAINS ON HER ANKLES AND WRISTS, is tugged to the auction block. A man sent to prison for his beliefs watches his guard close the cell door and fears that he has seen daylight for the last time. A soldier, hands on his head, is marched at gunpoint through the grim gates of his enemy's prisoner of war camp.

All very different people, from different times and places, and all dreaming of the same thing —

Escape!

It's an impulse every human being feels when trapped. No one is willingly confined, and every captive dreams of freedom. A special few will act on this slim hope.

Men and women have used their wits and courage to escape from all sorts of threats: from slave owners, from dungeons, from enemy armies, from physical danger. They may be fleeing jailers or governments. Some have been shut in by four walls, while other prisons are the kind you can't touch, but which trap people alive — in slavery or oppression.

The greater the obstacles to be overcome, the more impossible escape seems, the more the stories fascinate us. Across the ages, different places have come to mind as the ultimate challenges for escapers. Each era has had its notorious prisons — from England's Tower of London, where people who posed a threat to the government awaited execution, to France's Bastille, where inmates could be locked away their whole lives without a trial. Slavery — whether in ancient Rome or in many of the American states during the 1800s — was a fate millions dreamed of fleeing. The prisoner of war camps of the Second World War (1939–45), with their barbed wire, armed guards, and spotlights, seemed inescapable to all but a determined few. And the "Cold War" that followed, between the Soviet Union and the Western powers, brought with it the infamous East German border wall, which kept all but the most desperate defectors behind its barrier of concrete, mines, and armed patrols with orders to shoot.

And yet despite the odds, a few found ways past these deadly traps, ways that show the amazing range of human creativity. They got out with clever disguises or ingenious hiding places; by patiently waiting or boldly dashing forward; by using whatever materials were at hand, crafting tools of escape from even the most innocent-looking objects.

★ ★ ★

"I looked at my hands to see if I was the same person now I was free. There was such a glory over everything, the sun came like gold through the trees, and over the fields, and I felt like I was in heaven."

Harriet Tubman, an American slave who escaped from her master in 1849, remembered her first thrilling taste of freedom. Her reaction is surprisingly similar to the feelings recalled by other escapers, whatever the place and time. Many speak of the same exhilarating moment when, though they could scarcely believe it, they were actually free.

Once Harriet Tubman made it north to freedom she wasn't content to stay there, however. Despite the dangers, she returned south again and again to help other slaves escape, more than three hundred in all. She became part of the network of antislavery helpers known as the Underground Railroad, people who hid runaway slaves on their journeys north out of the slave states, often all the way to Canada.

Still, escape from the slave states was no easy matter. Often thousands of miles had to be crossed, with professional slave catchers close on runaways' trails. But until the Emancipation Proclamation freed all slaves in 1863, many were desperate enough to try. One slave even had friends package him inside a wooden box, three feet by two feet, and mail him to the state of Pennsylvania, where slavery was illegal. He spent 27 hours inside, and no one paid much attention to the label: This Side Up, With Care. Amazingly, he survived, and Underground Railroad workers unpacked Henry "Box" Brown, as he became known, in Philadelphia.

Some people have managed to escape all on their own, without aid, but many others could not have been successful without the bravery of secret helpers on the outside. The Underground Railroad was the most famous of such networks in the 1800s. A hundred years later, the Second World War saw the birth of secret organizations dedicated to helping Allied soldiers escape or evade capture by the enemy.

★ ★ ★

"It is every officer's duty to escape..."

An Allied combat pilot of the Second World War faced huge risks every time he climbed into the cockpit. If shot down, he hoped to bail out and parachute to safety. But even if he survived the landing his troubles were only beginning. His mission had probably taken him far over enemy territory — maybe Germany or occupied France. Chances were he'd been spotted on the way down, and enemy soldiers were already rushing to take him prisoner.

Military intelligence in England realized how critical it was to get these pilots, as well as the soldiers stuck in prisoner of war (POW) camps, back into action. A new branch of the British Secret Intelligence Service — dubbed MI9 — was formed. Its job was to do everything possible to keep downed pilots out of enemy hands and to help prisoners of war to escape. Working round-the-clock, the people at MI9 came up with gadgets and schemes to stay ahead of the enemy. The "science" of escape was born.

One unconventional technical officer at MI9, named Christopher Clayton-Hutton, realized that many escape tricks had already been discovered — by the soldiers of the First World War. Clayton-Hutton recruited schoolboys to read memoirs from World War I for clues to what a soldier needed in order to escape. He was impressed by the boys' work. Many of the ingenious escape methods of the previous war had been forgotten.

Clayton-Hutton scanned the boys' list of escape aids, and came across "dyes, wire, needles, copying paper, saws, and a dozen other items, some of which I should never have dreamed of."

He set to work on an "escape kit" that every pilot could carry in the front trouser pocket of his uniform and that held essentials to keeping him at liberty: compass, matches, needle and thread, razor, and soap (looking grubby was a sure giveaway when you were on the run!). Food was provided in small, concentrated form: malted milk tablets or toffee.

MI9 also wracked its brains to help prisoners of war escape their German camps. Getting out was hard enough, but once outside a crucial item was needed if they hoped to stay free — a map. Escaping POWs hoped to cross the German border into Switzerland, a country that had remained neutral in the war. From there they could make contact with helpers and get home.

But without a map, they were more likely to be recaptured while wandering near the border, lost. And it couldn't be just any old map. It had to open without rustling (escapers often consulted maps while search parties were combing the area nearby), and it had to be readable even when wet, and no matter how many times it was folded and creased. MI9 hit upon the solution: reproduce maps on silk.

But how would they get them to the prisoners? All POWs received mail from home, so MI9 came up with ways to sneak the maps in through letters and packages from "relatives." Working with the music company HMV, they inserted thin maps inside records, which would be sent to prisoners by nonexistent aunts.

As the war continued, MI9's tricks got cleverer. POWs were sent blankets that, once washed, revealed a sewing pattern that could be cut and stitched to make a German-looking jacket — a perfect disguise. The razor company Gillette helped to make magnetized razor blades that worked as compasses. Wires that cut bars were smuggled in shoelaces, screwdrivers inside cricket bats.

The stories of the lucky Allied soldiers who escaped from Germany were kept secret for many years, and important details were changed in or left out of books published after the war. Many people feared that a new war with the Soviet Union was on the horizon, and it would be foolish to give away escape tricks and routes that might prove useful during the Cold War. After all, a known escape trick is a useless one.

It was the Cold War that gave rise to one of the most famous symbols of imprisonment, and of the dream of escape: Germany's

Berlin Wall. This concrete barrier, topped with barbed wire and dotted with watchtowers and arc lamps, was begun by the Communist government of East Germany in 1961 to halt the flow of thousands of citizens defecting to West Germany. Soon the entire country was split in two by the border wall. In East Berlin some people could look out their apartment windows and see into the homes of West Berliners living on the other side. And yet they were completely cut off from one another. As one border guard put it, even though the other side "was only six or seven meters away I would never go there. It would have been easier to go to the moon. The moon was closer."

Although many residents of East Germany accepted their government and living conditions, others found they could not. Freedom — the freedom to travel, to say and write what they believed without fear of punishment — beckoned. Until the wall was torn down in 1989, countless escapes were attempted at the wall, and many died trying to get across it to the West. They tried climbing over it, tunneling under it, driving past it hidden in the cars of West Germans. Once again, it seemed that the bigger the obstacle placed between a person and freedom, the more human creativity is inspired to meet the challenge.

★ ★ ★

Imagine for a moment that you have been taken prisoner. You and your fellow captives are marched in a long line toward barracks behind barbed wire. As you file along the winding path leading to the compound, the guards at the head of the line suddenly disappear around a corner. You twist your head around. The guards bringing up the rear are also momentarily out of sight as you round the bend. For this one instant, you won't be spotted if you dive out of line and roll under the bushes along the path. You have mere seconds to make up your mind. What do you do? Stay in line and face the misery — but safety — of captivity? Or seize the moment and make a break for it?

Anyone in your place will dream of escape, but only a few will act on the impulse. MI9 estimated that far fewer than one percent of Allied prisoners of war took the plunge and escaped in World War II. But who? What kind of person?

Psychologists have found that people who escape often share the same character traits. They're not necessarily the strongest or the boldest, but they are open-minded and flexible — people who can improvise on the spot and adapt quickly to changes. If one tactic fails, they try another. They are willing to take risks and learn from mistakes. Often they are good actors, able to blend in with locals and to hide their fear or their intentions. And they're not the type to freeze when placed in a difficult situation, as many people do. They can keep a clear head and not panic. Perhaps most importantly, they firmly believe that their future survival depends on themselves, and no one else.

Pierre Mairesse Lebrun, a French cavalry lieutenant imprisoned by the Germans in World War II, felt that in some ways the personal bravery needed for an escape was even greater than that needed for the battlefield: "I think it's easy to be brave in war, unless you are a complete coward. Escaping is a voluntary act of bravery, which is very difficult. Very difficult when you are risking your life."

Lebrun himself certainly had his share of courage. Using his friend's cupped hands as a stirrup, he vaulted over his prison camp's barbed wire fence in plain view of the guards. Under fire, Lebrun dashed for the outer wall, bobbing and weaving like a hunted rabbit. He waited until the guards stopped to reload their guns, then scrambled over the second wall. Even his enemies had to admire his nerve: "For sheer mad and calculated daring," wrote the camp's German security officer, "the successful escape of ... Pierre Mairesse Lebrun, will not, I think, ever be beaten."

Perhaps not, but it certainly faces some tough competition. What follows are ten stories of real people who refused to give up their dreams of escape, no matter how huge the struggle.

Some are stories of people born into slavery, but who dreamed of freedom. And of those whose freedom was taken away from them, but who fought to win it back. Sailors kidnapped by slave-traders and dragged across the Sahara. A man captured in his homeland by the army of ancient Rome and condemned to fight to the death as a gladiator. A family that took to the air to cross a wall that seemed to have sprung up overnight, dividing their country in half and holding them prisoners in their own land.

These are dramas from across time and around the globe. From medieval knights trapped with their lady in a castle under siege, to modern diplomats who slipped through the fingers of captors in an embassy hostage-taking that shocked the world. From political prisoners who found ingenious ways out of some of history's most feared prisons, to soldiers who hatched a bold plan to break out of Germany's "escape-proof" camp, and a fighter pilot who faced every airman's worst nightmare — being trapped alive in a crashing plane.

All true stories of human courage, but also stories of hope — because hope is what kept these remarkable people going in the face of the most overwhelming obstacles and dangers.

Breakout from the Bastille

Paris, France, 1754

A GUARD PEERED THROUGH THE SMALL HOLE in the heavy wood door. With a sigh he watched the prisoner inside — writing again! This flood of letters, begging for his case to be reviewed, was a nuisance. The guard let the metal flap slam over the hole and walked away, shaking his head. Henri Latude could write until doomsday, he thought. It would come to nothing.

Inside the cold cell, the prisoner rubbed his ink-stained fingers to warm them. Blinking wearily, he angled his sheet of paper into the shaft of light streaming from a small chink in the stone wall. He had been locked up in the Bastille for five years without a trial, put away by a *lettre de cachet* — a piece of paper that let officials arrest someone in the King's name and keep him in prison for as long as they liked.

A foolish prank had landed him here. Like countless young men, Latude had left the countryside to seek a career in Paris. But that expensive city soon gobbled up his savings, and he could barely pay the rent on his tiny room. Favor at the royal court must be the key to success, Latude brooded. Why, people from backgrounds humbler than his had been raised to positions of honor by making the right impression there!

Latude came up with a scheme to gain favor with Madame de Pompadour, the close friend of King Louis XV. People said she was the real power behind the throne. They also said that she was terribly afraid of being poisoned or attacked by her enemies. Day and night she kept doctors and antidotes to poison at her side. She would never be the first to taste any dish.

That gave Latude an idea. What if he were to warn her of an attempt on her life and save her? She would be so grateful — surely she would promote him to some high office for his actions!

Latude bought four glass toys that would break with a bang when the ends were snapped. He sprinkled them with talcum powder and bundled them in a package. The outer wrapper was addressed to Madame de Pompadour. On the package inside he wrote, "Madame, I beg you to open this in secret." Smiling excitedly, Latude put his harmless toy bomb in the mail.

Then he rushed to court and begged to be allowed to see Madame. He had overheard a plot to send her a bomb!

The detective assigned to the strange case had his doubts about this loyal informer. He asked Latude to write down what had happened. Sure enough, the handwriting on Latude's statement matched the writing on the package.

No one laughed at Latude's prank. Perhaps he really had meant to hurt Madame, but was too foolish to do it properly. And surely he hadn't acted alone — this must be part of a larger plot. When Latude finally confessed to his little plan, no one believed him. The *lettre de cachet* did the rest.

Once the Bastille's heavy doors slammed behind him, Latude felt as if he had been buried alive. Since childhood he had heard stories of Paris's notorious prison, and they had filled him with dread. Its eight huge towers, linked by stone walls, cast a gloomy shadow over the Saint-Antoine district. No one seemed to know what went on behind those walls: any prisoner lucky enough to be released was sworn to silence about life inside. But the rumors were enough to terrify Latude's young imagination. It was where dangerous people — traitors, political enemies of the King — were locked away. And never heard from again.

And so he wrote letter after letter, asking for mercy, for justice. Most importantly, he begged those on the outside — Don't forget me! He wrote to the prison governor, to the chief of police, to ministers, to Madame de Pompadour herself. Letters were his lifeline to the outside world, and he clung to them.

At first prison officials mailed his letters. Then as time passed — and no one answered him — Latude's letters got stranger. He sent one minister an envelope full of cut-out letters of the alphabet, asking him to put them together himself in whatever words would move him to pity. Prison censors wondered, Is Latude going mad?

The governor of the prison ordered that Latude's ink and paper be taken from him. To the governor's horror, Latude kept writing — on a torn piece of his shirt, in his own blood.

★ ★ ★

Everything changed when Latude was given a roommate — Antoine Allègre, another troublemaker. The police hoped that putting the two men together would get them talking. Maybe they would let slip some new information about their crimes.

The result was surprising: Allègre and Latude started behaving themselves. The flood of letters stopped, as did Allègre's shouts and violent outbursts. Bastille officials sighed with relief.

What they never suspected was that Latude and Allègre had given up on letter-writing and screaming at the guards for a reason. They had a new idea now, and it filled all their thoughts. Escape.

A spark of hope Latude hadn't felt in years took hold of him. All the same, doubts preyed on his mind. Everyone knew that escape from the Bastille was impossible — wasn't it? Maybe I'm going mad after all, he thought.

He kept his fears to himself, as he and Allègre went over all the possible exits. Their room was on the fourth floor of one of the Bastille's eight towers. There was no getting out through the cell's heavy double door. It was locked with iron bars, and guards were right outside, day and night. They had one tiny window, but it was too small for a child to squeeze through, never mind a grown man.

And even if they could fit inside the window opening, four sets of iron grids barred their way through the six feet of stone wall. What's more, guards constantly checked the grids to make sure they were solid.

"The only way left is up," Latude said, half-joking.

Latude and Allègre raised their eyes to the chimney over their fireplace — in winter it barely kept the prisoners warm in the damp tower. Guards didn't search it often, since it was always filthy and smoke-filled.

Allègre stuck his head in the fireplace and peeked up the chimney. He quickly ducked back out and, brushing the soot off himself, shook his head. It was at least 30 feet to the top, and high up he could see layers of iron gratings, blocking the way.

"We could pry them out, one by one," Latude suggested.

"With what? We have no tools," Allègre answered. "And say we did, and could climb all the way up. We'd be at the top of the tower. How would we get down? It's at least an 80-foot drop — straight into a moat! Not to mention the huge wall on the other side of that."

Latude counted off the obstacles on his fingers. They would

need to make tools to remove the gratings. Plus ladders and ropes to climb up the chimney and down the tower wall, then to climb over the wall on the far side of the moat.

And guards were always listening in at the door, surprising them with searches. They'd have to build everything in total silence, then hide it in a flash. Latude and Allègre looked around the nearly empty room and at its meager furniture. All of it was regularly searched.

"Where would we hide everything?" Allègre asked.

They both fell silent. That was where their talk of escape always ended. They had no answer.

★ ★ ★

Latude and Allègre lay on their cots, staring at the ceiling. Latude listened to the prisoner above pace back and forth, the floor creaking with every step. "What a racket," he grumbled. "Why doesn't he just sit down?"

Allègre didn't answer at first. Then his eyes widened. He sat up. "But listen to the prisoner below."

Latude shook his head. "I can't hear a thing."

"Neither can I," answered Allègre. He paused. "But in my last cell, I could hear the man above me *and* the man below me."

"But there's someone down there," said Latude, sitting up. "I saw him myself on the way back from chapel."

So why couldn't they hear him?

"There's only one explanation!" Allègre whispered excitedly. "There's a space between the ceiling of the cell below and our own floor!" They both knew what that meant. A hiding place!

At 6:30 p.m. the guard brought their supper. The prisoners lowered the hinged table from the wall and ate in silence. As the food was taken away, Latude and Allègre exchanged glances. They knew no one would disturb them until morning. The guards were settled in their routine, and the two men were model prisoners now.

As soon as the door closed, Allègre and Latude began to wrench off the iron hinges that held the tabletop when it was down. They had their first tools! All they had to do was take their meals on their laps from now on and leave the table up.

With his hinge Allègre pried up one of the floor tiles, and the two men began to scratch at the mortar beneath. For six hours they scraped, barely noticing the aches in their arms and backs. Latude wiped his brow and glanced up — it would be dawn soon. The first guard of the day would arrive at five a.m.

Suddenly Allègre's tool pierced through the mortar. Latude joined Allègre as he scrabbled in the dust, clearing it aside. Allègre peeked through the hole, then motioned to Latude to do the same. Latude had to stop himself from shouting out loud. There *was* an empty space between the floor and the ceiling below — and it was at least three feet deep.

Allègre replaced the tile and carefully dotted mortar around it. No one would be able to tell it had been moved.

The two men collapsed onto their beds, exhausted. But Latude's head was spinning with happiness. He knew they were taking on a near-impossible task — and it would be painfully slow. But what did he have, other than time? From now on it was all he would think about by day, and toil at by night.

Each evening after the guard left they set to work. First they ripped the hems of their shirts and unraveled the threads, winding them into balls. Then they carefully braided the threads into a rope. As the rope grew longer, it began to eat up everything they could lay their hands on — shirts, underwear, stockings and breeches, napkins. As winter wore on, Latude and Allègre shivered half-dressed in their cell. They even unraveled the edges of their bed sheets, carefully stitching the hems back up and hoping the laundress wouldn't notice that their linen was getting smaller!

And before each dawn they hid it all under the floor, carefully laying the tile back in its place. The guards shrugged when the prisoners began napping during the day. It must help them pass the long hours, they thought.

Next they needed steps for their ladder. Each day they saved a bit of the wood the guards brought for the fire, and stashed it in their hiding place. At night they filed the logs into rungs — as quietly as they could.

Latude fitted the rungs one by one onto the rope, and laid out the 20-foot ladder for inspection. "Eighteen months' work," he said, stretching his back.

"Time for the chimney," said Allègre, nodding. Latude groaned — this would be the hard part!

"You first," Allègre smiled. "You're the nimble one."

Latude rolled up the ladder. Tucking it under one arm, he ducked through the fireplace and wedged himself inside the narrow chimney. He tossed the ladder up over one of the bars high above and climbed up to the first layer of gratings. Hanging in the gloom, he reached out to scrape at the cement around the grids, nearly losing his balance at first. His hands chafed on the rough stone and began to bleed.

An hour later he couldn't take it anymore, and scrambled down to give Allègre a turn.

Slowly, painfully, they pried out the chimney gratings one by one, and climbed a little higher. Each time Latude pried a bar loose, he gently placed it back in its hole on the way back down. You never knew when guards would inspect the chimney. But it was ready to be plucked out when the moment came.

And after hiding their tools each morning, Latude scanned the room for any sign of their work — the smallest chip of mortar could give them away.

★ ★ ★

Latude wound a strip of cloth around yet another rung. It had taken them six months to clear the chimney and braid a safety rope, and now he was halfway through the second ladder. This one would need at least 150 rungs to reach down the outside tower wall. Wrapping it in cloth was Allègre's idea — that way it wouldn't scrape noisily against the stone.

As he worked, Latude finally voiced the question that had been on his mind for months.

"What about the outer wall beyond the moat?" he blurted out. It was the most dangerous part of their exit route. Sentries patrolled the top all night long.

Allègre paused before ripping another strip of material. "There's only one way. We'll have to go through the wall — not over it." He handed the cloth to Latude. "We'll chip away the stones once we're in the moat."

Latude lowered his eyes, saying nothing. The doubts that had haunted him now made him turn cold. Could they do it? With a sentry walking over their heads? Maybe this was turning out to be madness after all.

★ ★ ★

Daylight was just piercing their small window as Latude slipped the last rung of the long ladder in place. He stared at it. He had thought it would go on forever! When he looked up at Allègre, he saw tears in his eyes. After seven years as a prisoner — eight for Allègre — Latude could scarcely believe this moment had come.

It was February 25, 1756, the day before Mardi Gras. The winter nights were long and dark, the river around the Bastille was high, and fog made it hard to see very far. There would never be a better time to escape. They would go that night.

The day seemed endless, but at last the guard came with their dinner and left. Latude hastily packed what clothes they had left in a watertight case. If they made it across the moat they would be soaked. And wet clothes would surely give them away in the city, if not freeze them to death first!

Allègre pulled the long rope ladder from its hiding place and began to piece it together, rung by rung. He counted as he went — 151 steps in all. They hauled everything over to the fireplace.

The prison bell tolled eight o'clock. Time to get going! As agreed, Latude began to climb up the chimney first, wedging his hands and feet against the sides, pulling out the iron gratings as he went. Let's hope it's for the last time, he thought. As he climbed, breathing hard, the chimney's walls seemed to press in on him. He grimaced as the rough stone rubbed the skin off his knees and elbows. Blood trickled from his elbows to his hands, making them slip.

Almost there, he told himself. Soot stung his eyes and made him choke.

At last he grasped the chimney top. Pulling himself up with his arms, he popped his head out into the air. The cold night wind blew on his face, and it felt delicious. He was outside! With a big push Latude hoisted himself out and sat astride the opening. He looked around at the foggy night — perfect! In the distance, a band played a march.

Latude lowered a cord back down the chimney, and the two

men worked fast to haul up their equipment — including two iron bars pulled from the chimney. At last Allègre sent up the short ladder, and Latude let it dangle down so the heftier Allègre could climb up.

Once Allègre had clambered to the top, the two men quickly scaled down the chimney's outer wall, landing on the platform between the towers. Latude glanced around through the fog — no sentries! He and Allègre pulled the long rope ladder down after them, and began to roll it up. All together, the pile of rope and wood was huge — nearly five feet high. Struggling under its weight, they carried it to the neighboring Trésor Tower, which they had agreed offered the best route down.

The two men tied the long ladder to a cannon and together they heaved the rest of it over the edge. Latude's stomach lurched as he watched it drop noiselessly down the side of the tower and disappear into the moat far below. He closed his eyes for a second to steady himself.

Allègre had already started rigging the safety rope to the cannon. It was 360 feet long, and Latude recalled how they had braided it inch by inch. Strong winds swept across the platform as Latude fastened the rope around his thigh, and he was glad they had been so careful. If the wind knocked him off the ladder, the safety rope would be his last hope.

With a nod to Allègre, Latude lowered his foot over the edge and onto the first rung of the ladder. He felt as if he were stepping into an abyss. Gripping the rope sides, he waited for his fear to pass, and then moved down rung by rung. Above him, Allègre fed the safety rope as he went. The wind whipped at his back in the darkness, and the ladder began to sway, brushing against the stones. Latude closed his eyes and held on. When it stopped rocking he took another step.

A sudden gust blew the ladder away from the wall and Latude felt himself swinging in midair like a kite, before falling against the stone again. He peered down into the blackness beneath him. It seemed to spin under his feet. Quickly he looked up again, and the dizziness left him. Step by step he kept going — down 80 feet of sheer wall.

When his foot touched the mire at the edge of the moat, Latude breathed a silent prayer of thanks. Allègre passed down the case and tools on a rope. Then, tying the safety rope to his own waist, he took his turn on the ladder. Latude pulled with all his might to secure the rope from below.

Once Allègre was at his side they peered across the moat. Latude could make out the silhouette of a sentry on top of the wall. As Allègre had predicted, they would have to do it the hard way — using the iron bars from the chimney to force a hole in the wall, which was four and a half feet thick.

Warily, they stepped down toward the water. Latude braced himself for the cold — but the shock was worse than he expected! They waded forward through the dirty, icy water, deeper and deeper. Soon they were up to their chests.

Once across, Latude got out their crude tools and began to pierce a hole between two stones. Suddenly a flash lit up his hands on the wall. He glanced up — the sentry was coming toward them along the wall top, swinging his lantern. Latude and Allègre sank down into the water to their chins, and listened to his footsteps pass over their heads. As soon as the steps died away, Latude stood up and kept scraping with all his strength.

The iron bar broke through the mortar, and Allègre was instantly at his side. They wedged in both iron bars and struggled to pry the stones loose, sinking down each time the sentry passed overhead.

Latude's hands and feet started to numb. They worked fiendishly, but their progress was slow. Too slow! Panic washed over Latude when he tried to guess how many hours had passed. Dawn was not far off, but he could not work any faster. A clumsy scrape of his bar or a splash of stone in the water would easily be heard by the patrol above.

As their hole grew, stones and debris rose in a pile above the water. Latude glanced up — the sentry was coming back. They sank down, splashing as they fell against the pile. The sentry's footsteps stopped.

Latude and Allègre froze. Had he heard them? Above, there were a few more footsteps as the sentry moved to the edge of the wall. Latude clenched his teeth to stop them from chattering. He wished he could sink underwater, but didn't dare — the splash would signal where they were.

He's right above us, thought Latude. Has he seen us? What is he doing?

A stream of water hit the top of his head. Latude nearly jumped out of his skin. Then it dawned on him — the sentry had stopped to relieve himself! Latude forgot to be disgusted. A few seconds later, he heard the sentry's steps again as he backed away from the edge and walked on.

After what seemed like an eternity, their hole reached the other side of the wall. As quickly as they dared, they pulled away the broken stone to make the opening big enough to fit through.

Allègre squeezed through first. Latude pushed the case after him. As he grabbed the stone sides to pull himself through, he glanced up. The sky was lighter now. How many hours had it taken them to break through the wall — six, seven, maybe more? Daylight was practically upon them.

Latude hurled himself through the opening. In his blind rush

he barely noticed the jagged stones that scraped his frozen skin.
Every second counted now.

One more moat lay between them and the road. Latude tested
the slope with his feet, and realized with horror that it was much
steeper than the first one, and the water much deeper.

He and Allègre looked at each other. Neither of them could
swim! But there was no going back. Side by side they plunged
down the bank into the icy water. Latude soon lost his footing on
the steep bank, and the water rushed over his head. He groped
blindly forward. Suddenly he felt Allègre thrashing wildly near

him, then gripping him in panic, pulling him down. Latude's mind raced frantically — he hadn't come this far only to drown!

With a kick he freed himself of Allègre. Then, with flailing arms, he grasped a root on the opposite bank. Reaching back into the water, he felt Allègre's hair and closed his fist around it, pulling him up. The two men gasped for air, clinging to the slope. Latude spotted a large object floating away — the case of clothes! He reached out and grasped it by the edge just before it moved out of reach.

They scrambled up the bank and collapsed onto the road above. Panting, Latude looked back at the stone walls looming behind them. *Behind,* he thought with sudden joy. They were outside! Free!

In the distance a church bell sounded five o'clock. Shivering, Latude fumbled to open the case. He could have wept with happiness — it was dry inside! Forcing their frozen limbs to move, he and Allègre tore off their wet clothes and pulled out the dry ones. With stiff fingers, the two men struggled with the clasps and buttons.

Then, in the pale light of morning, they set off down the rue Saint-Antoine, free men.

★ ★ ★

Latude stared into his empty coffee cup, now and then glancing up through the café window. Across the street, he could see the post office. A dozen times he'd made up his mind to get up and go in, but still he remained rooted to his seat. Would the police be waiting for him there?

He'd been on the run for nearly three and a half months. Allègre had escaped out of France first, disguised as a peasant.

He'd sent Latude a message telling him he was safe in Brussels, confident that the French police couldn't touch him in an Austrian domain. Latude had followed him there, but soon learned that Allègre had been arrested. So he *wasn't* safe, even outside France. He fled even further, to Holland this time.

Now he watched the people come and go from the Rotterdam post office, not far from the city's bustling seaport. In desperation, he had written to his mother in France, asking her to send him money under a false name. By now her letter would be waiting for him. He wondered if he had been foolish.

But if I had the money, he thought, I could go so far away they'd never find me. How big was the risk? Only a few seconds in a post office. He would do it.

His jaw set in a firm line, Latude stood up and strode across the street toward the office.

"A letter for Monsieur D'aubrespy?" he asked the clerk.

"Just a moment, sir."

Out of the corner of his eye, Latude saw a figure move. Then a hand clapped on his shoulder. Before he turned around, he knew it was all over.

★ ★ ★

Latude lay on a bed of straw in a dungeon deep beneath one of the Bastille's towers, shackles on his wrists and ankles. Moat water seeped in and soaked the floor. Rats roamed fearlessly, eyeing his rations of bread and water.

By the winter of 1781, Latude's letters were no longer sent to anyone.

With a few coins he'd managed to scrounge, Latude bribed a guard to take one last letter to a councilor at Parliament. But the guard carelessly dropped it outside in the snowy road, forgetting all about it.

A woman trudged through the snow on an early morning errand. She spotted something in the slush at her feet and stooped to pick it up.

It was a letter. Water had erased the address. Madame Legros turned it over — the seal was broken. She peeked inside for an address so she could deliver it.

Her eyes ran down the desperate plea for help on the page inside. She raised a shaking hand to her mouth as she read the long signature: "Masers de Latude, prisoner for 32 years at the Bastille, at Vincennes, and now at Bicêtre, on bread and water, in a cell 10 feet underground."

Forgetting her errand, Madame Legros raced back to the small shop she ran with her husband.

It was two years before Latude saw the woman who was working to free him. Madame Legros knocked on the doors of anyone she thought could help, pleading with their servants to let her in for a few moments.

Surprisingly, a few people did let this unknown woman inside, and listened to her story. Word spread of her cause, and she found more and more supporters — some of them powerful. When the queen herself was moved to pity, it was only a matter of time. On March 23, 1784, King Louis XVI issued a new *lettre de cachet,* this time freeing Latude forever. He was given no apology or reason for his long imprisonment without trial, only a small pension, which he used to live with his new friends, Madame and Monsieur Legros. He had been a prisoner for 35 years.

Five years later, the Bastille was stormed by an angry mob. The French Revolution had begun, and the downfall of France's monarchy and ruling class was close at hand. For revolutionaries, the Bastille was a symbol of power used badly. In 350 years it had held nearly 6,000 prisoners. Only seven ever escaped.

Days after the storming, revolutionaries began to tear down the massive prison, stone by stone, while crowds of people watched. One them was Latude.

"From here there is no escape..."

Germany, 1941

COLDITZ — THE NAME WAS ENOUGH to send a chill through the boldest prisoner of war. During the Second World War, the Germans turned this medieval castle into their greatest *sonderlager:* the highest-security, most heavily guarded camp for captured enemy soldiers. Hermann Goering, Hitler's second in command, had personally declared the camp absolutely escape-proof. Here the Germans sent the troublemakers from every other prisoner of war camp — especially those determined to escape. As the war raged on outside, Colditz was home to hundreds of Allied soldiers — Polish, British, Canadian, French, Belgian. And in 1941, they were joined by 68 Dutch.

"For you the war is over," the new prisoners were told by the German guards who herded them through the castle gates at gunpoint. As the young Dutch lieutenant Hans Larive looked around him, it wasn't hard to believe. During their march through the town below he had admired the fairy-tale castle high on a cliff. But that illusion disappeared with a closer look. Inside, the castle's high, gray stone walls blocked the sun. Glancing up from the damp courtyard, he spotted pale faces peering down through the barred windows all around him.

"*Appell!*" barked a German officer — time for roll call. The Dutch snapped to attention, forming neat ranks in the courtyard.

With sideways glances they watched the other prisoners drift in. One by one they came, or ambling in pairs. Some wore torn uniforms ragged from battle, some were half-dressed — one seemed to be in his pajamas! The Germans' frustration mounted as they tried to impose order, but every time they thought they'd finished counting they spotted an officer wandering out of his place or lined up with the wrong nation.

Larive was surprised by the chaos, but then slowly he understood the game the other prisoners were playing. Keep the guards frustrated and confused: it was a kind of psychological war. The French and British seemed to be the worst offenders of all. He watched as the British were lined up closest to the armed guards — obviously this was the "bad boys'" place during roll call. The Germans seemed to eye the Dutch with relief. They were so disciplined and quiet — at least there was one country they didn't have to worry about!

Or so they thought. From the moment Larive arrived he watched for a chance — any chance — to get out. He had to rejoin the fighting! But as the days passed he learned that this was no ordinary camp. Everything about Colditz was a cruel reminder that escape was out of the question. Constant roll calls made sure no one was missing. Prisoners and their quarters were searched day and night. There were as many guards as prisoners, and they kept the inmates in check with guns and bayonets, with searchlights to spot them, microphones to listen in on them, dogs to sniff them out.

And yet one thing kept Larive's hopes alive — the memory, still fresh in his mind, of a strange twist of events that had followed his capture. After escaping from another German camp, Larive had been caught near the border of neutral Switzerland. He was then taken for questioning by a Gestapo agent, a huge bull of a man who began by shouting threats. But when the agent had learned that Larive was Dutch, he relaxed. He had worked in Holland before the war and liked it there.

"The only clever thing you did was to get off the train at Singen — all the rest was stupid," he had told Larive.

"Why?"

"You must have known that Singen was the last station where anyone could get off the train without showing an identity card."

In fact, it had been a lucky guess. The "Bull" had then asked Larive why he hadn't just walked across the border.

"I didn't know how to get through the defense line," Larive admitted.

"Defense line!" he stormed. "Defense against whom? The Swiss? What a crazy idea. There are no defenses at all. You could have walked straight across."

To Larive's amazement, the Bull even got out a map and showed him where the Swiss border jutted into Germany, and the road he could have taken to walk across it. How could he talk so carelessly? Larive wondered. Then he realized: of course, the Germans believe they will soon win the war. Where I'm going there's no hope of escape, and I'd be a fool to get shot trying. Larive had nodded and listened — and memorized the map.

★ ★ ★

Larive settled into the prison's dreary routine, but he kept wondering if there wasn't more than met the eye at Colditz. He watched officers milling about the courtyard, lying on their bunks. So much time on their hands, he thought — surely enough time to plan escapes.

He had guessed right. Colditz was a maze of a castle, and Larive soon heard rumors of out-of-use passages and hidden rooms where prisoners worked on one scheme after another — from tunnels to disguises. The place is seething with escape plans, Larive realized, his pulse quickening at the idea. In fact there were so many in progress that the different "countries" began to cooperate so they wouldn't mess up one another's schemes by mistake.

Larive and the other Dutch wasted no time fitting in. They would need to choose a leader for their own escape "team." The obvious choice was the burly, quick-minded Captain Machiel van den Heuvel, whom the British quickly nicknamed "Vandy." It was an important job, but there was a catch. The escape officer was not allowed to escape himself — he would mastermind escapes for others, and always stay behind. Vandy accepted.

Larive and Vandy soon discovered that the Germans had made a mistake when they locked up all the troublemakers in one prison. Now every kind of escape artist — from lock pickers to explosives experts — was in one place. Some had gained valuable experience on their failed escape attempts. Larive was one of them.

Vandy was all ears as Larive told him in hushed tones the story of his capture and questioning by the Gestapo. Now the Dutch at Colditz knew a way across the border, but how could they get out of the castle? That was the puzzle Vandy set his mind to. The outer walls were monstrous and heavily guarded. But prisoners had one opportunity to be outside the walls — even if it was under an armed escort. The key had to be "the walk."

Exercise was impossible in the castle's cramped courtyard. And so the prisoners were regularly marched to a nearby park surrounded by a high fence. The guards knew this was the weakest point in their security and grumbled about the extra trouble it caused — the manpower needed to take the prisoners back and forth, plus all the roll calls before, during, and after to keep track of the men.

It was also a prime opportunity for the prisoners' favorite pastime — annoying the guards, or "goon-baiting." When called for the walk they would show up slowly one by one, then drop things and stroll back for them. Vandy knew the Germans were glad that at least the Dutch didn't stoop to these games. They were always orderly and easy to count. That could be useful too, Vandy mused.

As Vandy strolled around the park, he noted the armed sentries along the fence, the barbed wire, the guard dogs. He sighed and looked down. What he saw at his feet made him pause — a cement square set into the ground, covered with a wooden lid. It was shut with a heavy nut and a bolt, and dotted with small airholes. He quickly looked up and kept walking before the guards could see what had caught his attention. But his mind was racing.

On the next trip to the park, Vandy casually sat down on the wooden lid and pretended to watch the prisoners' rugby game. Never moving his eyes from the players, he reached into his pocket and pulled out the pebble he had tied to a long piece of string. Slowly he fed it through one of the small airholes. How far down would it go? He lowered it further and further. Two feet, three feet, four, five — *plop!* The pebble hit water. So it was an old well! He lowered it further, and it dropped another five feet or so before hitting the bottom of the well. Perfect! Vandy's expression didn't change, but he was so pleased it was hard not to smile.

In the days that followed, the German guards shrugged when they noticed the Bible study club Captain van den Heuvel had started leading during the exercise hour. What was the harm? Sitting quietly in a circle, always on the same spot, the men were easier to track. It also served Vandy's purposes nicely. With the well hidden from view, he set to work measuring the nut and bolt, making plans, barely hearing the voices that droned on around him.

Hans Larive walked aimlessly around the park, too anxious to join in the rugby, too restless to sit down. The waiting was driving him crazy. Nights ago, he had helped prepare two Dutch officers for their escape, drilling them on the route to the Swiss border. He knew the escape plan concerned the well in the park, but he was puzzled. The well was a dead end, so how did they get out? The scheme appeared to have worked, but Vandy had not let him in on the details, not yet. He kicked at the dirt. When would his turn come? On the grass, a shadow lengthened and moved toward him. Looking up, he saw the large form of his escape officer striding toward him, a smile on his broad, ruddy face. Before Vandy spoke the words—"Are you ready?"—Larive's answer was already on his lips, a confident "Yes."

On a hot August afternoon, Larive took his place in line to march to the park. Ahead of him he could see his friend Flanti Steinmetz, the other Dutchman who would make the break today. Almost every Dutch officer had a role to play. Vandy had gone over each man's part and had stressed the obstacles to be overcome. Somehow Larive and Steinmetz had to get into the well unseen by the guards. Then the guards and their dogs must be kept from closely searching the grounds, even though the Dutch would be two men short at the roll call that ended the exercise hour. And the Germans must stay confused for as long as possible to let the escapers get a head start.

Once at the park, every man took his place. Far from the well, several of the Dutch began a noisy game of rugby. The bored guards turned to watch. Larive and Steinmetz, meanwhile, joined a circle of officers who were lazily throwing a ball to one another across the well cover. At the same time, Lieutenant Gerrit Dames settled down against the fence between two guards and quietly read a book. Another officer strolled aimlessly along the barbed wire. The minutes passed.

Vandy gave the agreed-upon signal. This was it! The circle around the well started closing in. The rugby game got rougher and noisier than ever. The officer near the fence began to pull playfully at the wire like a naughty schoolboy. And Dames, still looking at his book, began to slowly cut a hole in the fence behind his back.

Finally, a guard lost his temper at the Dutchman playing with the wire, and his angry shouts caught the attention of the other guards. Screened from view, one of the officers around the well dropped to the ground. From his pocket he drew the homemade wrench Vandy had built over many nights, sized just right to loosen the nut and bolt on the well cover. Working fast, he removed the bolt and passed it to Larive, who stashed it in his pocket. The shouts of the guards continued in the distance as they led the troublesome officer away from the fence.

In a flash, the lid was lifted and Steinmetz slipped into the darkness below, followed by Larive. Above them, their helper closed the lid and put the finishing touch in place. It was Vandy's small stroke of genius. He smiled as he gently centered the new "bolt" — a carefully painted piece of glass that looked just like the real thing, but would smash easily when the lid was lifted from inside.

By now Dames had finished cutting his hole in the fence. He turned around and, with clumsy slowness, began to creep through. As expected, a guard's whistle pierced the air. Dames shouted toward the woods beyond the fence, "Run, run!" He felt the barrel of a rifle at his back and, slowly drawing his head out of the hole, raised his hands in the air. Seconds ticked by. Dames exhaled heavily — they weren't going to shoot.

A quick count of the prisoners was taken in the park. Two men missing! The German guards combed the park with their dogs, but found no one. They gave the well cover a quick glance, but it was clearly undisturbed with the bolt still in place. Their suspicions were confirmed: the two men must have escaped into the woods before the guards had spotted the third man, Dames. The Dutch were marched back to Colditz, while a widespread search of the woods began.

"*Sonderappell!*" Back in Colditz castle, the other prisoners weren't surprised by the shouts announcing a surprise roll call. A common nuisance. But as they streamed into the courtyard they noticed the atmosphere was tenser than usual. Guards were rushing back and forth, commanders talking in small groups. Then whispered rumors began to make their way through the ranks of prisoners. It's the Dutch... someone is missing! The British officers nearest the guards strained to overhear. No, make that two men. Wait a minute, I think it's more... four, five... *seven* missing? Impossible!

The Dutch group was marched in at gunpoint. All faces turned to look at them, but as usual their dignified expressions gave nothing away. The lines of prisoners made way as the Dutch were marched past their usual place in the courtyard. Then the guards ordered the British and French ranks to stand aside. A cheer went up through the prisoners as Vandy and his countrymen were led straight to the bad boys' place nearest the guards. Applause and whistles echoed through the courtyard, but the Dutchmen looked calmly ahead.

In fact, seven men weren't missing, but four were. Vandy had succeeded in tricking the guards. Two men had left through the well days ago, and the Poles had helped Vandy make up the numbers at roll call. Now, while Larive and Steinmetz hid in the well, three more men were hiding in the castle itself to help confuse the guards. Vandy knew the Germans' Operation Mousetrap would spring into action. Rail and police stations in the area would be alerted, and guards would scour towns and roads for miles around the camp, quickly spreading a net to catch the escapers. But they would be looking for seven men, not two. And those two weren't running to a station or town, not yet. They were hanging inside a well under the feet of the guards looking for them.

Vandy wasn't finished with the well, either. He wanted to get two more officers out fast, before the Germans found it, before they'd expect another attempt. He knew he couldn't use the fence trick twice, so the "third man" was out. Vandy stared straight ahead, barely hearing the German officers shouting around him. His mind was already forming a new scheme. His thoughts went back to the fake glass bolt he had painted. And to his friends in the Polish group, particularly one who was a sculptor. And to how appearances can be deceiving, especially when there's something you expect to see.

★ ★ ★

Larive's arms ached and his back was sore from crouching. For hours he had been hanging from the iron rungs on the side of the well, half of his body underwater.

At first he and Steinmetz had crouched on the rungs, but they realized that if the guards opened the lid they'd be seen immediately. Quietly, they had lowered themselves into the water, then draped a gray blanket they'd brought over their heads. If things went wrong and the guards opened the well, they'd see a gray mass — maybe they'd think it was the dirty water below and move on.

Hanging in the darkness, they listened to the guards' whistles and shouts above their heads and the sound of running feet. Then dogs barking in the distance. A murmur of voices nearby, growing fainter. And finally silence. Hours passed. The lid had closed over their heads at three o'clock, and it wouldn't be safe to come out until nine or ten, when darkness forced the Germans to call off their search for the night.

Time crawled by slowly. Larive's head was splitting and it was getting harder to think straight. He tried to take a deep breath, and his lungs heaved slowly with the effort. He watched Steinmetz's chest move up and down, as if he were panting.

"We are breathing like fish on land," Larive gasped. And then he realized why — not enough oxygen. They were slowly suffocating!

Steinmetz dragged himself up the rungs toward the lid. Slowly he pushed it open a crack and, careful not to break the glass bolt, propped it up with his pocketknife. He and Larive put their mouths to the opening and drank in the fresh air.

Outside, dusk was turning to darkness. They peered out the narrow opening. No lights, no sounds. It was time. They pushed up the lid, smashing the glass bolt as planned. Steinmetz hopped out and picked up the broken pieces, while Larive fished the real bolt out of his pocket and replaced it on the closed lid.

Quickly scrambling over the fence, they walked and crawled toward the nearest rail station, hoping to catch the first train at dawn. It was a gamble. Police would already be looking for anyone suspicious. They'd have to count on the civilian clothes they had faked and Steinmetz's perfect German to help them pass as tourists.

Luck stayed with them all the way to Singen — the last train stop before their walk to the Swiss border. As they set out along the dirt road that ran next to the tracks, Larive had an eerie sense of coming home. He had traveled the same road after his last escape — and had landed in front of the Gestapo. In his mind he went over the Gestapo agent's words: "Did you see where the road split from the tracks? An hour more of walking, a left turn through some fields, and the border would have been straight ahead of you."

The road veered from the tracks and led into the woods. Remember, Larive told himself, the Bull said there's no defense line. But he couldn't shake a feeling of dread as they entered the forest.

Then, rounding a corner, he saw something that turned his

blood cold: a German guard up ahead, moving toward them along the same side of the road. Larive and Steinmetz slowed down. What now? If they turned back, he'd suspect them for sure. Maybe he wasn't there to check papers.

"Let's cross the road," Larive whispered. "If he crosses, too, we'll know he means to check up on us."

Casually they strolled to the other side of the road.

"He is crossing!" Steinmetz exclaimed under his breath.

A few steps ahead Larive saw a narrow path heading off the road through the trees. But it led away from the border! No choice now. The guard was closing in and picking up his pace. "Turn right up the path — and run," Larive whispered. The two men bolted.

"Halt!" they heard the guard shout from behind. Larive forced his tired legs to move faster.

A shot was fired, and a bullet whistled past Larive's head. They dove off the path and kept running through the trees, the leaves and branches whipping their sides and faces. Larive waited for another shot but none came. He slowed a little to look back. No guard. He's gone back to raise the alarm, thought Larive. The two men slowed down and circled back, creeping from shrub to shrub to the edge of the woods. Crouching deep in a thicket, they watched the road.

Across a field they could see some commotion at a distant guardhouse. The sky grew darker and Larive felt a few drops of rain. Good, he thought. The harder the better. It will make us tough to spot tonight. Soldiers were now leaving the guardhouse and taking up posts along the road. The road they needed to cross to get to Switzerland! Suddenly, rifle shots made Larive jump. Then loud barking. The hunt had started.

"They're trying to scare us into running, so the dogs will hear us and pick up our trail," Larive whispered. He and Steinmetz sunk further into the thicket and covered themselves with their blanket. Their best chance was to stay quiet and perfectly still.

The barking grew louder and voices were getting clearer. More shots, closer this time. Larive's heart was pounding as he willed himself not to move, not to breathe too loudly. The guards' footsteps were very close now. This is crazy, thought Larive. Even if they don't see us they'll step on us! Then slowly the voices became dimmer, the barking moved further off. Soon only the rain falling on the leaves broke the silence.

Darkness came, and the two men crawled slowly out of the woods on their stomachs. Larive looked for some landmark to guide them, but everything looked the same in the pitch-black night. They found another dirt road, but was it the right one? They kept going. In the distance, Larive could make out the shapes of houses. That might be the Swiss village on the other side of the border. Or the town they had just left — were they going in circles? They passed signs but couldn't read them in the dark. Steinmetz climbed a signpost and struck a match before the words. In a flash, he dropped down. "German Customs!" he hissed.

Half running, half stumbling, they came upon a small group of houses. Were they Swiss or German? It was too dark to tell. Steinmetz leaned against a wall to catch his breath out of the rain. Larive joined him.

They discussed the situation in hoarse whispers. Maybe it was best to stay put and not get more lost. At dawn, they could get their bearings and make a final dash for the border. Larive leaned back. He'd never been so tired. Two and a half days on the run, without sleep and almost nothing to eat. His clothes were soaked and he felt cold and numb. Stay sharp, he told himself. This is when your mind dulls, and you do something stupid.

Suddenly the white beam of a flashlight stung his eyes, blinding him. He and Steinmetz froze, as if pinned to the wall by the light. Larive could hear the sound of boots squishing in the mud, coming closer. But he could see nothing beyond the glare of the light. Then a voice confirmed his worst fears — it spoke in German.

"Who are you? What are you doing here?"

Tears stung Larive's eyes. Not again! They couldn't be more than a few hundred yards from the border. Then anger replaced his exhaustion. No, he thought. I won't go back this time.

The beam of light moved to Steinmetz and back again. Behind it, Larive glimpsed a soldier with a rifle strapped across his back. It would take a few seconds for him to grab his weapon and aim.

Larive whispered to Steinmetz, "We must kick hard, both at the same time, then run. I'll say when." Steinmetz nodded grimly.

As the soldier came closer, they slowly lifted their right legs and pushed their hands against the wall behind them.

"Where did you come from? Are you prisoners of war?"

Larive took a deep breath. As he opened his mouth to say "Now!" the voice spoke again.

"You are in Switzerland. You'll have to come with me."

It took a moment for the meaning of the words to sink in. They were free.

★ ★ ★

In a corner of the Dutch quarters at Colditz, Vandy frowned as he inspected the two dummy heads from different angles. At last, he stepped back and gave a grunt of satisfaction. They were remarkable! His Polish friend had outdone himself. The amateur sculptor had modeled them out of plaster — obtained from a castle repairman who was always willing to take a bribe. The faces had then been painted by a Dutch lieutenant, who had snuck paints from a prisoners' art class.

Attached to frames, draped with long Dutch coats, and topped with officers' caps, the dummies — which the Dutch nicknamed "Max" and "Moritz" — were ready for action. Two more officers were about to escape through the well in the park. While they made their run for the border, Max and Moritz would stand in for them at roll calls, hiding their absence for as long as possible.

Vandy had noticed that the guards now took a shortcut when counting the Dutch prisoners. The orderly Dutch always stood in neat rows of five. The guards simply counted the rows, and so many rows times five gave them the right number. During the noise and confusion before roll call, while the British and French were stalling and goon-baiting, the Dutch walked out in a large group. They tucked Max and Moritz in the center, held by the officers on either side, who slid two extra pairs of boots under the dummies at the last minute.

It worked brilliantly — for a time. Months after the well escapes, a suspicious German guard took a closer look at the Dutch.

He raised his hand. "All from here to the right, move to the right. All from here to the left, move to the left," he ordered.

As the prisoners shifted position, one was left alone in the middle. The guard pointed at the prisoner with the blank expression and repeated his order. No response. The guard stormed toward him, and his anger turned to astonishment. Max had been found out. But Vandy didn't mind — by this time his two escapers had followed Larive and Steinmetz to freedom in Switzerland.

★ ★ ★

Escape attempts continued at Colditz, some ingenious, some out-rageous — through a trapdoor under the theater stage; hidden in garbage; disguised as German officers, workers, women. In a secret attic room, the British even built a glider to carry escapers over the castle's high walls to the valley below. The glider never had a chance to take flight, however. It was found by the amazed American GIs who liberated the castle in 1945.

Through Traitor's Gate

London, England, 1716

IT WAS NEARLY EVENING AS A LADY, wrapped in a cloak, her face almost hidden by her riding hood, stepped down from a horse-drawn coach onto the cobblestones. She looked up for a moment at the gray stone walls that rose before her, then lowered her gaze and strode ahead with a determined step. As she passed through the arched gateway, the sentry gave her a fleeting look of sympathy, but his face quickly hardened again into its usual cold stare. He was sorry for her troubles, but her husband was a traitor, after all.

The lady shivered as she made her way forward. Was it her imagination, or was it really colder, the air stiller, now that she had stepped inside the walls of the Tower of London? Ahead, across the small green, rose another stone wall. High above, she could see slits in the stone — tiny windows that lit the cells inside. Silently she counted the slits and found the one that cast its dim light on the room where her husband waited for her. And for the day of his execution.

It was out of family loyalty that William Maxwell, Lord Nithsdale, took up the doomed cause that had brought him here. In 1715 a plot was hatched to replace King George I with the exiled James Stuart. Many nobles, especially Scottish ones such as William, believed that James was the rightful heir to the throne.

And the time seemed ripe for swift action — the people were grumbling about the German-speaking King George, who knew little English and showed even less affection for his British subjects. William joined his friends and allies in a march south to England, rallying support along the way.

Their rebellion was over within the year. Surrounded and defeated at Preston by King George's forces, the rebel lords were led through London's streets on horseback, their hands tied behind their backs, past the jeers and shouts of the crowds. Soon afterward, the disappointed Stuart prince fled back to France, where he had been living in exile.

Three Scottish lords were found guilty of treason and sentenced to death — their heads to be cut off with an axe. Once sentenced, they were thrown into separate cells inside the Tower of London, the gloomy stone fortress that for centuries had held traitors and notorious criminals within its many dungeons. There the men were to stay until their executions.

★ ★ ★

In the frozen garden outside the family manor in Terregles, Scotland, Winifred leaned on her spade and surveyed her handiwork. Her palms were blistered from the shovel's handle, but she paid them no mind. It had been only a few hours since the news of her husband's death sentence had reached her at home in Scotland. She had choked back her tears. There was too much to do.

Quickly she had buried the deeds to the family lands in the garden. Her son would need them someday to claim his inheritance — without them all their property would be seized by the king. Snow would cover the hiding place soon enough.

Brushing the dirt from her hands, she next took a hard look

at the facts. William had pleaded guilty. The date for his execution was set — February 24, only days away. Things looked grim indeed.

But one hope remained. She'd race to London herself, and beg the King for mercy.

Winifred set out at once to hire a stagecoach, but none dared to travel in the heavy snowstorm that blocked all the roads. If she would just wait for the storm to pass, the drivers offered. But Winifred knew that every day was crucial. Very well, she decided, her jaw set stubbornly. I'll ride on my own.

Winifred and her trusted maid, Evans, mounted their horses and set off at a gallop for London — hundreds of miles away. Through the day and past nightfall they rode south, stopping to rest only when they were too exhausted to go on. The weather grew worse, and the horses shied from the sharp winds and deep snow ahead. With grim determination, Winifred dismounted and called to Evans to do the same. Together they walked through the waist-high snow, pulling their frightened horses forward by the reigns.

At last they staggered into London and found lodgings for the night. There, sympathetic friends tried to reason with Winifred. It was hopeless. She must accept it: William and the others would have to die as an example to all traitors. But Winifred shook her head.

The next day she asked for an audience with the king, but was turned away. Unwilling to give up, she dressed in black mourning clothes and went to St. James's Palace, planting herself in a corridor where she knew the king would pass. There she waited. And waited.

After what seemed like an eternity, a bustle of activity made her look up. There he was — the king! — striding in her direction, surrounded by attendants. Winifred wasted no time. Blocking his way, she knelt before him, and began to plead her cause. But he just brushed her aside and kept walking.

Winifred struggled up and followed him — in a moment he would be gone, taking her hopes with him. Squeezing through the attendants, she tried to push her written petition into his pocket, but it fell to the floor. Tears began to blind her, but this was no time to worry about dignity. Just before he moved out of reach, she lunged forward and grabbed his coattails. The angry king strode on, dragging her behind.

Gasps could be heard all around as horrified royal attendants rushed toward her. No one could touch the king! Soon firm hands were pulling her away. She stood up and shook them off, but it was too late. The king was gone. And with him goes any hope of a pardon, thought Winifred.

Which left only one other way.

★ ★ ★

As Winifred passed under the Tower archway, walking toward the stone Lieutenant's Lodgings where her husband was locked up, her eyes took in everything — the sentries along the green and at the entrance, the two flights of stairs, and at the top the grand Council Chamber full of warders, the Tower guards. Across the guardroom was the heavy door to William's cell.

Before it stood a warder armed with a halberd. With a nod, he opened the door for Winifred. She smiled sweetly and slipped a generous tip into his hand.

Inside, William rose swiftly from his seat and stepped forward, grasping Winifred's hands in his. After their heartfelt reunion, Winifred listened patiently as William paced the floor and spoke his mind. He was resigned to his fate and was ready to face execution with dignity, without flinching, so his family could be proud of him. He had even written his final words.

Winifred, however, had other ideas. She began unfolding her plan. William's room was high in a stone tower, its door well guarded, its only window a mere slit in the stone 40 feet above the ground. What's more, the cell door opened onto a crowded guardroom. There was no hope of sneaking out or jumping.

"But there is another way..." Winifred paused. She'd have to lead up carefully to the crucial part. "You could walk out in plain view of the guards, disguised — only for a few moments mind you — as a visitor... a lady visitor—"

William raised a hand to silence her.

He was a proud man. To face the axe was one thing. Walk up the scaffold with a steady step, looking bravely ahead — yes, he believed he could do it. He would do it for honor's sake. But to be caught sneaking out of the Tower in a dress!

"Can you imagine the laughter, the sneers? No," he said, folding his arms. "My family would never live down the shame. No."

"But that is if we fail, and we won't!" Winifred cried. She spoke passionately, quickly explaining the rest of her scheme.

William listened in silence. She'd thought of everything, there was no doubt. It was clever, he admitted. And it was one last chance for life.

When Winifred had used up all her arguments, she sat back, waiting breathlessly for his answer. William stood for a while with a hand on the stone wall, looking down. When he looked at her again his eyes were gleaming. He would do it.

★ ★ ★

Winifred poured the afternoon tea into porcelain cups, her movements calm and delicate. She waited a moment before raising her eyes. When she did, her maid and their landlady, Mrs. Mills, were both looking at her expectantly. Winifred took a breath, silently running through the phrases she had rehearsed in her head all morning. She prayed they would be persuasive enough.

Then in a flood of words she told the ladies everything. Her husband was not going to be pardoned. Tomorrow he would be executed. There was only one chance left — to help him escape, tonight. Everything was ready. But she needed their help. Would they do it?

Evans readily agreed. Winifred smiled and squeezed her hand. Then she turned to Mrs. Mills. Winifred knew she was loyal to the Stuart cause. But would that be enough?

Their landlady was dumbstruck, clearly astonished. Winifred bit her tongue as she waited for her answer. Had she been right to spring the idea at the last minute like this? She had hoped that the surprise and urgency would keep the women from considering the danger. At last Mrs. Mills nodded mutely.

They would need one more helper. Who else could they trust? Evans quickly sent for her friend Miss Hilton, and Winifred's dramatic pleas won her over as well.

Her accomplices in hand, Winifred moved fast. She ushered the three women outside and into a waiting coach, which she had arranged beforehand. Throughout the ride she kept chatting — that way no one would have a chance for second thoughts.

Her scheme sounded complicated, but it was based on a very simple idea: to confuse the guards with women coming and going from the prisoner's room.

"For days before an execution, all men visiting the Tower are stopped and challenged to identify themselves," she explained.

"But not the women! And what coldhearted guard would stop a grieving lady, crying as she said farewell to a prisoner for the last time?"

As the speeding coach lurched and bumped over the stone roads, Winifred reminded each lady of the part she would play. Mrs. Mills was a large, tall woman, and a few months pregnant. Lady Nithsdale had noticed that with her pregnant belly she was just about the same size and shape as her dear William! It was as "Mrs. Mills" that William would make his walk to freedom.

Miss Hilton, on the other hand, was tall and thin, and could easily wear two riding cloaks, one over the other, without looking suspiciously bulky. Winifred cast a critical eye over the lady and was satisfied that no one would guess she was smuggling in a disguise.

The sun was low in the sky as the coach pulled up alongside the Tower's arched entrance. Weaving through the stream of Tower workers still coming and going, the women headed for William's prison house.

"Prisoners are allowed only two visitors at a time," Winifred told them. Leaving Evans and Mrs. Mills at the foot of the stairs, she guided Miss Hilton up to William's cell.

The warder before William's door straightened and stepped forward as the two women approached. Winifred knew that for their plan to work, she would have to break the Tower rules — on the night before an execution, the prisoner's wife could visit only if she stayed with him until morning. That would ruin everything! She linked arms with Miss Hilton and strode forward, praying that the tip she had given the guard the day before had done the trick.

On cue, Miss Hilton began to sniffle and sigh, but Winifred, in a loud voice, told her not to fear. "At this very moment the king is considering my petition for a pardon. All will be well, Mrs. Catharine!" she said, adding the lady's first name for everyone to hear.

Turning to the warder, she added, "I am afraid I must leave after seeing my husband tonight. I have an audience with His Majesty."

The warder's face softened, and he nodded slightly as he opened the door. The other guards exchanged glances, then looked down. Her hopefulness was touching, but they knew there wasn't much chance of a pardon.

As soon as the door closed behind them, Miss Hilton slipped off her top riding cloak, and William tucked it out of sight. The two women waited anxiously for a few moments, and then walked out together.

In a worried voice, Winifred called for her maid. There was no answer. She called again, and the guards turned their heads toward Winifred. As they listened to her shouts they scarcely noticed the quiet Miss Hilton slipping past and down the stairs.

Winifred continued to cause a scene. "Pray send up my maid at once to help me dress — it is nearly time to present my last petition to the king!"

Below her, the stout Mrs. Mills was already huffing on her way up the stairs. Winifred took her by the arm and lead her past the guards toward the cell. As planned, Mrs. Mills pressed her handkerchief to her face and sobbed loudly the whole way. The guards looked away, embarrassed. Good, thought Winifred. The less closely they look, the better!

Lady Nithsdale smiled and patted her friend's arm, saying loudly, "I have high hopes, Mrs. Betty, that the king will pardon my husband this very night."

Inside William's room, Mrs. Mills took off her cloak and put on the one Miss Hilton had left. She handed her own cloak and handkerchief to William. Then she straightened up and prepared to walk out with her head held high.

"No crying this time," Winifred reminded her. "You must look like a different lady than the one who went in with her face in her handkerchief."

Winifred led her by the hand into the guardroom. Glancing around, she noticed that the room was fuller now. The guards' wives and daughters were sitting in small groups, whispering. After all, it wasn't every day that three executions were to take place at once!

A hush fell as the two ladies passed, their footsteps echoing under the high, timbered ceiling. Winifred turned to the disguised Mrs. Mills and addressed her as if she were Miss Hilton.

"My dear Mrs. Catharine," she said with growing alarm in her voice, "go in all haste and send me my waiting-maid, she certainly cannot reflect how late it is. I am to present my petition tonight, and if I let slip this opportunity I am undone, for tomorrow will be too late."

From the corner of her eye Winifred could see the looks of pity on the ladies' faces. "Hasten her as much as possible," she called after Mrs. Mills as she hurried down the stairs, "for I shall be on thorns till she comes."

Winifred turned and walked back toward William's cell, noting with satisfaction that the guards on either side looked away as she passed. Inside his room, William had already put on Mrs. Mills's riding cloak. Now it was time to complete the transformation!

Winifred fished out the tools she had hidden under the folds of her clothes. First she must do something about his heavy, dark eyebrows — Mrs. Mills's were a light sandy color. She brought out the paint she had prepared and began to disguise them. Next she fitted a light-haired wig over his head. With quick, sure strokes she powdered his face and painted his cheeks with rouge, to help hide his stubbly beard — he'd had no time to shave! Over it all she pulled the hood of his cloak, close around his face.

Finally, she stepped out of all of her petticoats except one and slipped them under William's cloak.

Winifred glanced up at the small window and noticed it was growing dark. This was the time she had planned for their exit — in the twilight that would hide their faces, but before the candles were lit.

They stood together before the closed door, blocking the rest of the room from view. Winifred turned to William and raised her eyebrows.

He nodded and pressed the handkerchief to his face. As Winifred pulled the door open, William began to make loud sobbing noises. Holding his hand, Winifred stepped out and guided William through the doorway.

The murmurs in the guardroom died down as they appeared.

"Evans has ruined me by her delay!" Winifred said for all to hear. "How could she do this to me?"

They started walking, past the guards and their wives. Only their footsteps and William's sobs broke the silence. The guardroom seemed endless, and Winifred felt the ladies' curious eyes boring into them. Was she walking too quickly, too suspiciously? She took deep breaths to slow her racing heartbeat.

"My dear Mrs. Betty," she said to William, her voice catching and sounding tearful, "for the love of God run quickly, and bring her with you. You know my lodging, and if you ever hurried in your life, do it now. I am almost distracted with this disappointment."

They were halfway there now. William kept his face buried

in the handkerchief, his head turned into Winifred's shoulder.

At the far end of the room servants were starting to light the candles. Winifred held her breath — a moment more and the room would be brilliantly lit. She picked up her pace.

Not so fast, she scolded herself. The heavy oak door was right before them now. Only a few steps more.

Suddenly a guard sprang forward, blocking their way. Winifred stopped in her tracks, and tightened her grip on William. She felt the blood drain from her face. They were trapped!

The guard bowed slightly and opened the door for them, his face full of sympathy. Winifred tried to hide her relief. She began to steer William through the door toward the long staircase flanked by sentinels. Not far now.

As William passed before her through the door she nearly gasped in horror. He was walking like a man! Dress or no dress, it was a miracle no one had noticed before now. She grasped him by the elbow and pushed him in front of her. They moved forward awkwardly, with Winifred's wide skirt hiding William's masculine walk from the sentries.

Past the guards, down the stairs, on and on Winifred begged anxiously — "Please hurry and send my maid." All the while, William cried loudly in his handkerchief, never daring to raise his eyes and counting on Winifred to steer him. The sentries stood aside to make way for them, the sympathy on their faces turning to exasperation.

All these women, all this weeping and calling after maids. Such a ruckus — there must have been three or four of them at least — or was it more? They felt sorry enough for the ladies, but this was getting tiresome. If only they would just leave!

At the bottom of the stairs stood Evans, and the sight of her loyal face steadied Winifred's nerves. She handed William over,

and Evans led him across the green toward the outer gate.

Outside the Tower walls, Mrs. Mills's husband was waiting for them. His wife had convinced him to help by having a safe house ready for the fugitive, but he had doubted very much that the women would succeed.

Now, there they were — Evans and Lord Nithsdale coming toward him through the archway! Mr. Mills was so astonished that he forgot what he was supposed to do. Surprise and joy crowded out every other thought, and he stood rooted to the ground, gaping. A few passersby slowed down and stared curiously at the group.

Glancing around, Evans saw the attention they were attracting. Time to take things firmly in hand, she thought.

Hailing a coach, the maid quickly pushed William inside and climbed in after him. She could sort things out with Mr. Mills later! Now they had to put as much distance between themselves and the Tower as they could.

★ ★ ★

Winifred walked slowly back up the steps and through the guardroom toward William's empty chamber. She had a final role to play out inside the Tower. She must buy time for William to get away — before the guards raised the alarm, before searchers flooded the streets and gave chase.

Again the warder politely let her into William's room. Winifred watched the door close behind her. She took a deep breath and began to talk to William as if he were still there. She paced up and down — as if they were walking together — to make it more convincing.

A sudden thought made her heart jump. They might wonder why they could hear her, but not him! She began to answer her own questions in his deep, quiet voice. All the while her mind was calculating — have they had enough time to clear the guards, cross the Tower green, and slip through the outer gate?

She kept up the illusion as long as she dared, then glanced outside at the dark night. It was time to make her exit as well.

Slowly she opened the door. Standing halfway out so that the guards could hear her words, but holding the door so close that they could not see inside the room, she bid farewell to her husband.

"Something unusual must have happened to keep Evans," she said. "She has always been faithful in even the smallest matters. But I can afford to wait no longer."

The guards kept their eyes discreetly lowered as she talked.

"I will go directly to the king now," Winifred said reassuringly. "My task completed, if I can still gain admittance to the Tower, I will see you tonight. But if I cannot, do not worry, my love. I will be here tomorrow morning as early as they will let me in. With good news, I trust," she added, smiling bravely.

Just before shutting the door, Winifred pulled through the string of the latch. Now it can only be opened from the inside, she thought with satisfaction, and there's no one there to do that! She gave the handle a sharp tug and slammed the heavy door firmly shut.

Turning to leave, she looked up and started in surprise. A servant was heading straight for her. He was carrying William's supper on a tray!

"My lord is praying now," she said quickly, stepping in the servant's way, "and does not wish to be disturbed. He has no need of supper or candles — he plans to fast until his pardon arrives." The servant nodded and turned away.

With a sigh of relief, the sentries watched Lady Nithsdale pass down the stairs and out into the night.

★ ★ ★

A few days later Lord Nithsdale escaped to Italy disguised as a servant on the Venetian ambassador's boat. Lady Nithsdale mounted her horse and rode back to Scotland, where she dug up the deeds for their lands. It was a risky journey for her. King George was furious about Lord Nithsdale's escape, and search parties combed the country for Winifred. The king swore that Lady Nithsdale "had given him more trouble than any woman in the whole of Europe!" But Winifred slipped through the searchers' fingers and joined her husband in Rome, where they lived near the court of the exiled Stuart family for the rest of their lives.

Fugitives in Iran

Tehran, Iran, 1979

THE CHANTING HAD DRONED IN THE DISTANCE since early that gray November morning. Crowds of student protesters were a daily sight outside the walls of the American embassy compound in Iran's capital. But now the voices were getting louder, sounding closer.

Set back from the main entrance, the fourteen Americans in the consulate building felt far away from the noise. They ignored the angry shouts and kept working, processing applications from Iranians for visas to study or travel in the U.S. The protest was not their concern, and no doubt the police would soon break it up. But a panicked cry from an Iranian secretary destroyed their illusion of security.

"They're inside the walls!"

Staff rushed to the window. The students had broken the main gate and were streaming into the compound. The grounds were filling up with people — young men in khaki fatigues, women in head scarves or the full-length black *chador* that covered them from head to foot. Some carried pictures of their spiritual and political leader, the Ayatollah Khomeini, on poles. Others were armed with knives, lead pipes, or guns.

"Stay calm." From behind, the voice of Sergeant Lopez, a young marine, sounded reassuring. "It could just be a sit-in protest."

They had all known something like this was bound to happen. Since the Shah, Iran's former ruler, had fled his country, Iranian revolutionaries had shown more and more resentment toward his American allies. The return of the exiled Ayatollah Khomeini — an Islamic scholar who believed the country should be run by clerics — had focused people's anger into a full-fledged revolution.

Walking through the city, the American diplomats had sensed the growing fear and suspicion — especially toward them. What were these foreigners doing in Iran anyway, the revolutionaries demanded. Trying to run our country for us? When President Carter had allowed the Shah into the U.S. for treatment at a hospital, tensions had reached a boiling point.

The sound of footsteps on the roof made everyone tilt their heads up. Seconds later they heard a window shatter in the washroom. Lopez rushed there just in time to push back a student trying to climb in from the roof. The marine fired a tear-gas canister out the window. Retreating quickly, he then wired the washroom door shut with a coat hanger and herded the staff and Iranian visitors further back into the building.

"How can this be happening? They can't do this to an embassy! We're diplomats," sputtered the shocked employees. The Vienna Convention of 1961 was supposed to guarantee the protection of ambassadors and their staff in foreign countries. The embassy and its grounds belonged to the U.S., and could not be entered without permission.

"Can't you guys do something?" someone asked the marine. Lopez shrugged. The guards were there to defend the staff, not attack anyone. It was another rule of diplomacy: embassies must count on the host government to protect them. "I can't fire on citizens of this country," he explained, "unless someone's life is in immediate danger."

Robert Anders, the senior diplomat in the building, took charge. "We'll barricade the doors and hold out until the police or the army arrives to restore order," he announced.

The staff huddled closer together. The group of visiting Iranians spoke little English, but the anxious looks on their faces showed they understood the situation. They were about to be caught in the den of the enemy by the most extreme of the revolutionaries. How would the militants deal with them?

Outside, the roar of the mob, now three to five hundred strong, was frighteningly loud. Over his two-way radio, Lopez learned that the main embassy building, the chancery, had already been stormed by the revolutionaries. But so far no one else was trying to get into the consulate.

"They've forgotten about us," Anders thought aloud. "For now."

Suddenly the room went dark. "The lights! They've cut the electricity!" Panicked voices filled the darkened room. Lopez talked rapidly into his walkie-talkie, but received no answer. He tried again. Still nothing.

His face was in darkness, but the others could tell how he felt by the grim tone of his voice. "They must have captured the other marines. We're cut off."

Slowly the words sunk in. The handful of staff understood: they were on their own.

"We've got to get out now, before they find us!" someone wailed.

"Our best chance is the exit on the north side," Anders reasoned. On the side of the building facing away from the demonstrators in the compound, a sliding door opened directly onto the street.

Two by two, the Americans and Iranians filed down the stairs toward the north door. Close behind Anders were two young couples: Joe and Kathy Stafford, and Mark and Cora Lijek. Lopez followed at the rear, locking doors behind them, buying time for their escape. He stayed behind on the ground floor to smash visa plates, so no forgeries could be made by the invaders. He would leave last — if at all.

At the north door, Anders raised a hand to signal everyone to wait. Slowly he slid the door open a few inches and peered up and down Bist Metri Street.

To his surprise, he saw no one. No protesters, not even any passersby.

"Okay, move out in small groups. That will attract less attention."

The Iranian visa seekers slipped out first, followed by Iranians who worked at the embassy. Anders led the Staffords and the Lijeks out next. The rest followed behind.

All was quiet outside, but for the heavy rain. They dashed down the wet street, the sounds of protest faint in the background.

"Where to now?" Breathless, Joe Stafford voiced the question on everyone's minds. The nearby British embassy was the safest bet, they agreed. But to avoid the protesters they'd have to stick to the back streets — a confusing maze of alleys in the ancient city. They'd be lost in minutes.

Most of the Iranians in the group were already out of sight, but one woman had stayed behind. "I can show you the way," she bravely offered. The Americans nodded, grateful. Picking up some newspapers to protect their heads from the rain, they began to weave their way though the alleys, turning their faces away whenever they passed anyone.

Coming out of a lane, they stopped across from the square that separated them from the British embassy. Their hearts sank: it was full of protesters.

The Americans slunk back into the alley. They thanked their Iranian guide, and she slipped away. One of the men urged them all to go to the house of the consul general. But Anders shook his head. It was too obvious a hiding place. And it would mean backtracking toward the American embassy, something no one wanted to do.

Unable to agree, the group split up. Five of them — Anders, the Staffords, and the Lijeks — began a long walk across the city to Anders's apartment. Creeping through the alleys, they arrived there by mid-afternoon, drenched and exhausted.

Anders quickly got on the phone, calling the homes of other embassy staff in the city — surely someone else had slipped out. But no one answered.

"Does that mean we're the only ones who got away?" Cora Lijek asked.

Growing frantic, Anders called every contact he could think of. Then, in the middle of a call, the telephone line clicked and went dead.

Anders slowly replaced the receiver. "Calls always get cut off in Tehran, it could mean nothing," he told the others. But they looked unconvinced.

Joe Stafford pulled out a radio, one that all the diplomats carried, and tried to contact the embassy. But on the crackling line they heard only shouting in Farsi, the Iranian language. The embassy was under the students' control.

Why hasn't the government sent in troops? Anders wondered. A sudden realization made him turn cold. Because they support the takeover, that's why. Or else they know they're powerless to do anything.

The five Americans looked at each other in silence. They were far from home in a hostile place, and a revolution had stripped away their last shreds of protection. Everyone was thinking the same thing: Where can we go?

★ ★ ★

Robert Anders was running out of ideas. The American fugitives had been on the run for days, moving from place to place. Revolutionary Guards were combing the city, picking up Americans on the streets and in offices. Anders and the others had spent a few days hiding with British diplomats, but their hosts grew uneasy, so they left. Servants had let them into the empty apartments of Americans trapped on the compound. But everywhere they had sensed they were being watched. At night they lay awake, jumping at every little sound. Sometimes they felt sure the servants were whispering about them.

Within hours of taking over the embassy — or the "Den of Spies" as the militants called it — the armed students released their demands to the media. They would hold the 60-odd trapped Americans hostage until the United States returned the exiled Shah to Iran to stand trial. If not, they would put the hostages on trial for spying.

To make matters worse, Iran's moderate prime minister, Mehdi Bazargan, had resigned. The country was now being run by the Revolutionary Council and the Islamic clergy it looked to for guidance — in particular, the Ayatollah Khomeini. There would be no help from such a government.

Anders knew the American government was in a tough position. Agreeing to the demands would not only mean handing over their ally for certain execution. It would be saying to the world, If you seize our embassies, we'll do what you want.

And where did that leave the five of them? Was it just a matter of time before they were dragged back to the compound to join the rest? That's what must have happened to Lopez and the others who'd split from their group. Anders was sure of that by now.

Desperate, Anders called an old friend — John Sheardown, Canada's chief immigration officer in Tehran.

"Why did you wait so long to call me?" Sheardown blurted out before Anders could finish his story.

The next day a car pulled into Sheardown's driveway, and inside the five fugitives sighed with relief. Finally a safe haven — for the moment, at least.

Sheardown quickly ushered them inside, where his wife Zena was waiting. Within seconds Canada's ambassador, Ken Taylor, arrived as well. When Sheardown had told Taylor about Anders's phone call, the ambassador had responded without hesitating: "Okay, where will we hide them?"

It was the kind of reaction Sheardown expected from his boss, who was energetic and unconventional, eager to cut through red tape to get to the heart of a matter. After a speedy coded message to the Ministry of External Affairs in Ottawa, Taylor got the official go-ahead to help the Americans.

As the fugitives gathered in Sheardown's living room, the Canadian ambassador went over the situation with them.

"We can't hide you at the embassy — downtown is too dangerous. So we'll be splitting you up. The Staffords will come to my house in the north of the city. The Lijeks and Bob Anders will stay here with the Sheardowns. No one will expect you to hide in our homes.

"How about extra security? Can any Canadian military be posted to the houses?" Sheardown asked.

Taylor shook his head. "No, that would only draw attention. It would give us away in a second. Life has to go on normally. No changes."

"But you must have Iranian staff at your homes — servants. Can we trust them?" Joe Stafford asked.

"We'll tell them you're Canadian tourists, friends of mine," Taylor said. "But you'll have to stay inside, especially during the day. You mustn't be spotted by the *komitehs,* the patrols who make the rounds of the neighborhood. Remember — stay out of sight."

After some hurried goodbyes, the Staffords left for the Taylor residence, and the Lijeks and Anders followed Zena Sheardown to their rooms. Cora carried all they'd brought with them in one small suitcase. They'd fled their last hiding place in such a panic, the clothes were still running in the washing machine.

★ ★ ★

Mark Lijek sat chin in hand, drumming his fingers on his cheek and staring at the Scrabble board. Now and then he glanced up at Cora, who sat across the coffee table, waiting for his move. Nearby, Anders was sunk in an armchair, reading a magazine. The silence in the house seemed to wrap around them.

I can't take much more of this, Mark thought. Reading, playing cards — it was all they could do to pass the long hours trapped inside the Sheardowns' house. For the first weeks they slept in, but still the days seemed endless. Mark and Cora were playing three hours of Scrabble a day! Cora had started running up and down the stairs to blow off steam. Anders had told them to pretend they were at a luxury resort, with a storm keeping them inside. But it hadn't helped. It's feeling so helpless and nervous, Mark thought, with nothing to take your mind off the fear — that's what's unbearable.

At Ken Taylor's house, the Staffords had the same cabin fever. Joe, who spoke some Farsi, listened all day to local radio, desperate for information on the hostages at the embassy and what — if anything — was being done to free them. What if the American government doesn't give in? he wondered. Will the militants start executing the hostages for spying?

Worst of all, he knew the Iranian staff at the Taylor home were getting suspicious. He'd overheard questions from the head servant and the cook — Why would tourists have so little luggage and never go out? They like to travel light, Taylor's wife, Pat, had answered. They're resting before they start sightseeing. But even to Joe the excuses sounded lame.

Then, a few weeks into their hiding, Taylor sprung some good news on them. Someone else had slipped through the students' fingers. Lee Schatz, an American attaché who leased space at the Swedish embassy, had been there when the takeover happened. He'd been hiding with the Swedes ever since.

The Swedish ambassador had called Taylor. Sounding apologetic, he asked if Canada could possibly hide Schatz — he wasn't likely to pass as a Swede, but he might have better luck posing as a Canadian. Taylor, with his mischievous sense of humor, had savored the moment. No problem, he'd told the shocked Swedish ambassador, we're already hiding five!

Schatz's arrival at the Sheardowns' gave everyone something new to talk about. As American Thanksgiving approached at the end of November, Taylor decided it was worth the risk to sneak Schatz and the Staffords over for a reunion dinner with the Lijeks and Anders. It would help keep everyone's spirits up. When the turkey was finished, someone joked, "Let's hope we're not all here for Christmas!"

There was silence around the table. That was a possibility no one wanted to talk about.

★ ★ ★

Ken Taylor went about his daily business, but it was getting harder with so much weighing on his mind. All through December he'd watched the Americans growing more restless and desperate. How much longer could he keep them a secret?

Some North American journalists had noticed that the original number of staff at the American embassy was greater than the number of hostages announced by the students. Where were the others? they asked. Government officials had asked them to keep it quiet, since lives were at stake, but sooner or later it was bound to leak out.

And rumors were spreading of a rescue operation. The U.S. military might storm the compound and whisk the hostages out by helicopter.

Then what would become of the six left behind? Taylor knew there'd be only one chance for an airlift — they couldn't fly back for the others. And the Iranian militants could argue that since the Canadians had been hiding them, the six must be spies, and as such had no diplomatic protection. They'd stay and stand trial, along with their Canadian accomplices!

Clearly, it was time for them all to get out.

Christmas came and went as Taylor weighed the options for escape. They could drive the Americans northwest to the city of Tabriz, then over the border to Turkey, where a helicopter could pick them up. Or take them west to the Persian Gulf and get them on a British tanker.

Both plans were risky, and they meant traveling through dangerous areas — some parts of the country had been plunged into even greater turmoil by the revolution than Tehran. Plus they would need safe houses along the way, and a Farsi-speaking guide they could trust.

No, Taylor realized, there was only one way. Confront the Iranians head-on. Take the Americans straight through Tehran's airport and onto a jet to Europe. It was the boldest option, but the swiftest, and the only one that stood a chance.

★ ★ ★

"Who is this?" A man's voice demanded over the telephone at the Taylor residence.

"Pat Taylor. And who is speaking, please?" Pat didn't recognize the voice, and an uneasy feeling told her to be careful what she said.

The man's reply turned her blood cold. "I'd like to speak to Joseph or Kathy Stafford. I know they're there."

Pat swallowed and answered steadily, "I don't know who you're talking about. There's no one here by that name." She glanced over at the Staffords, who had risen from their chairs and were standing nearby, watching wide-eyed.

The stranger began to argue with her, but Pat insisted he was mistaken. The man hung up suddenly.

Joe put an arm around his wife. This felt like the last straw in a series of scares that had tormented the Americans. Days before, a helicopter had mysteriously circled over the Sheardown home, terrifying Zena and the Americans hiding there.

Pat quickly phoned the ambassador, who rushed home. "Don't worry," Taylor reassured the frantic Staffords. "We're getting you out."

Taylor, together with officials in Ottawa and Washington, had worked out an escape plan. First of all, the fugitives would need new identities: Americans might not be let out of the country. But Canadians could still come and go.

Canadian Prime Minister Joe Clark had quickly issued six Canadian passports. For the next step, Ottawa turned to the Central Intelligence Agency in the U.S. They'd need the CIA's expert help to forge Iranian stamps on the passports, showing that the "Canadians" had entered Iran. And they'd need fake visas allowing them to enter and exit the country.

By mid-January the passports and visas arrived in a diplomatic pouch under the arm of a Canadian embassy courier. The CIA had also provided driver's licenses and credit cards to make the identities seem more real. As hoped, the pouch was not checked at the airport. Luckily some diplomatic privileges were still respected!

But when Taylor looked at the visas, he gasped. The dates were wrong! The CIA had followed the old calendar used by the Shah and not the Islamic calendar reintroduced by Khomeini. According to the visas, the Americans had arrived in Iran a month after they were leaving! Taylor said nothing to the hostages. His staff hastily doctored the date — and hoped it wouldn't show.

The last days before the escape ticked by in a nerve-wracking countdown. The plan was to leave during the national elections, when confusion throughout the city would help mask their departure.

On January 26, 1980, the night before the escape, Taylor sat down with the six Americans and the few remaining Canadian diplomats. Taylor knew the Canadian embassy's days in Iran were numbered, so staff had been leaving the country bit by bit, all the while keeping up the illusion that everything was business as usual.

Huddled in a circle, the Americans were handed their passports and began studying their new identities.

"You are a group of Canadian business people in the oil industry," Taylor explained to them as they eyed their new passports. "You came to Iran in early January, stayed with embassy staff, and are now returning home. Everyone ready? Let's start."

The Canadians began drilling the Americans on their new identities. Together they rehearsed every kind of question that might come up at the airport. Where was your visa issued? Where were you born? What was your business in Iran? The slightest hesitation before answering, a little confusion over details — any number of small blunders could give them away.

Next they studied a map of the airport terminal and its many checkpoints. Taylor showed them where they would run into police, guards, and immigration officials, and where their visas would be checked and double-checked. The toughest spot was about halfway through, at the third checkpoint — a barrier guarded by National Police and Revolutionary Guards.

Finally, Taylor circled the waiting area where they'd stand before boarding. "But don't relax once you're there!" he warned them. "You can't let your guard down until the plane is in the air. Even when you're sitting on the runway, Revolutionary Guards could board the plane for one last check of papers." The Americans nodded.

"Remember," Taylor added. "If one of you is arrested, the rest of you mustn't panic. Walk away — slowly — to the exit. Two cars will be waiting for you outside."

It was late and they all needed rest. Taylor stood up, wishing them luck. He wouldn't be with them the next day — if they all left together, it would raise suspicions.

He smiled on his way out, but silently he worried about the Americans. They'd done well in the mock interrogations. But they'd been cooped up for three months. They're healthy, Taylor thought, but dazed. Are they still sharp enough to react quickly to the unexpected? Because, as he knew, something unexpected was bound to come up.

★ ★ ★

At dawn the Americans piled into a car and prepared to face the many roadblocks on the way to the airport for their 7:35 a.m.

flight to Frankfurt, Germany. They arrived at the terminal without incident, but Anders was nervous. He had processed visas for so many Iranians at the consulate. What if someone recognized him?

One by one the travelers checked in their bags, then headed for the first of the security stations. At a distance, two Canadian diplomats strolled around the airport, watching their progress.

When the group reached the third checkpoint, the official stared at Schatz's passport, looked up at him, then back down. Suddenly he snatched it up and slipped out of sight into an office.

Don't panic, Schatz told himself. As moments passed and the man didn't return, Schatz raised his sleeve to mop the sweat on his brow. He sensed the others standing nervously behind him, but didn't dare make eye contact.

The official abruptly returned and held out the passport, his face expressionless. Schatz reached for it, tensing his hand to stop it shaking.

Mark and Cora's hearts were pounding as they strode toward the final checkpoint, where their visas would be examined. But no one was there. Mark and Cora hesitated. Should they just walk through? Mark eyed the departure gate, and was tempted to sprint toward it.

But Anders grabbed his arm to hold him back. If anyone spotted them, guards would be all around them in a second. Mark groaned as Anders went in search of help. I can't believe it: we're actually going out of our way to talk to guards, he thought.

But Anders had done the right thing. A nearby guard found the missing official, who apologized and waved them through.

The minutes ticked by slowly as they strolled around the waiting area. It's not over yet, Anders told himself.

A voice blared over the loudspeakers. Joe quickly translated the Farsi announcement — mechanical difficulties were delaying the Swissair flight. Panic spread through the group.

"What if it's just a ploy to stall us?"

"We're like sitting ducks here."

Twenty minutes went by. In low mutters, the Americans ran through Taylor's back-up plans. They could split up and catch other planes — each of them had a ticket for another flight, just in case. Or they could slip out of the airport and make a run for the safe house Taylor had rented as a last resort. It would buy them a couple of days, or at least a few hours.

"No, let's wait it out," Anders urged. "Bolting now would look suspicious."

An hour passed as they agonized. At last another announcement ended the torture: passengers were now boarding the Swissair flight. One by one, the fugitives filed past the Revolutionary Guards on either side of the gate and mounted the steps to the airplane.

Taking their seats, they stared anxiously at the door, watching for any sign of guards boarding at the last moment. The minutes passed and none came. The plane began to move along the runway, slowly picking up speed. As it lifted off the ground, the Americans felt themselves soaring. They were in the air! To the surprise of the other passengers, the six "Canadians" broke into tears and laughter. They were going home.

★ ★ ★

Once news of the escape broke, Americans said a big "thank you" to Canada. Towns and cities across the U.S. flew the Canadian flag, people pinned maple leaves on their lapels, and thousands of thank-you messages, as well as flowers and cakes, arrived at Canadian embassies.

But in Iran the crisis wasn't over yet. The embassy hostages still faced another year of captivity. A sympathetic guard showed a few of them a magazine story on the escape, and it gave them new hope. One hostage, worn out by months of confinement, blindfolds, and fear, later called the escape story "the most incredibly beautiful thing I've read in my whole life."

The U.S. military did attempt to rescue the hostages by helicopter, but the mission was a tragic failure, killing eight members of the rescue team. In the end it would take the sudden death of the Shah and a war with Iraq to spur Iran to negotiate a release for the hostages. The captive Americans came home on January 20, 1981, after 444 days as prisoners.

Falling from the Sky

England, 1941

IT WAS A PERFECT DAY FOR FLYING — a warm August morning with scattered clouds at 4,000 feet, and above them clear, blue sky. Into it rose three squadrons of Spitfire fighter planes, climbing steadily over the countryside, bound for the English Channel. The pilots' mission was to escort British bombers on their way to a German military target in occupied France.

In the air battles that had raged over the past year of the Second World War, England had pinned its hopes on the fast and nimble Spitfire. When the skies over England had darkened with squadrons of German bombers, the sight of a Spitfire sparked hope and defiance in those on the ground. Across the country, school kids had memorized its sleek outline, and would spot it at once, waving furiously as it soared overhead.

But on that August day, the weather was about the only thing going right. Wing Leader Douglas Bader had trouble with his radio from the start. Then, soon after takeoff, the needle on his airspeed indicator began to swing up and down, and suddenly dropped to zero. The mission needed precise timing — impossible if he couldn't tell how fast he was flying. Someone else would have to steer the group to its target. Bader handed over the job to one of his trusted pilots, "Cocky" Dundas.

Dundas wasn't alarmed. He trusted Bader's judgment and his

brisk, on-the-spot decisions. The pilots were a tight-knit group, with confidence in one another.

It hadn't always been that way.

★ ★ ★

Now it seemed like ages since the Royal Air Force pilots of 242 Squadron first heard they were getting a new commanding officer. Word quickly spread that he was a bit unusual — he had no legs. He'd lost them both in an accident. The pilots groaned.

"I don't suppose we'll be seeing much of him," they said, rolling their eyes. Just what they needed: a passenger, not a leader. A useless figurehead who would sit in an office.

They couldn't have been more wrong. In fact there was nowhere Bader would rather be than in the air, where his legs didn't matter. A pilot needed good hands and eyes, not feet. And ever since he joined the Royal Air Force at 18, he had lived to fly. Confident and energetic, he had been a bit of a show-off during his training — taking the plane through loops and rolls that were against the rules. But he was so friendly that people readily forgave him.

His RAF report said it all: "Plucky, capable, headstrong." His flying was rated as "above average," which satisfied Bader. The only higher rating was "exceptional," a mark so rare that it seemed mythical.

Bader learned a lot in his first two years, becoming confident in the air, maybe a little over-confident. His instructor had to lay down the law with him: no more stunts. He'd taken his instructor's words to heart, but his friends didn't let the matter go so easily. It wasn't long before he was asked to show his stuff in the air.

"No," said Bader firmly. The requests turned to needling. One sounded an awful lot like a dare, and that stung Bader. No one could say he was afraid. His mouth set in a grim line, he climbed angrily into a nearby biplane. While his friends watched, he took off and prepared for a strictly forbidden piece of aerobatics: a low roll close enough to the ground to silence any of his doubters.

He pushed the control column over and the plane began to roll to the right as he sped forward. Now the wings were vertical... halfway there.

And then the plane began to drop. Upside down, Bader struggled to complete the roll. Suddenly the left wing hit the grass, bringing the plane's nose down. The plane cartwheeled and plunged into the dirt, smashing the propeller, sending the engine flying. Bader blacked out.

Later, he'd heard the doctor say, "I'm afraid we've had to take off your right leg," but the words didn't mean anything — not yet. Through the haze of pain that followed he learned that the left leg had to go as well, because infection had set in. And once, while in a dreamlike state, he heard a nurse outside his hospital room hush a noisy orderly: "Shhh! Don't make so much noise. There's a boy dying in there."

A shock ripped through Bader. He opened his eyes. That's what *they* think! The challenge kept him going, through his recovery, through the pain of learning to walk on artificial legs. He'd been offered a cane, but stubbornly threw it away. "Never!" he snapped. "I'm going to start the way I mean to go on."

It was a long road back. "I *know* I'll still be able to fly," he'd said, but the RAF didn't agree. He settled down to a desk job. It was 1933.

Six years later, England was at war. Germany's massive, highly trained air force — the Luftwaffe — would soon be poised in occupied France. Thousands of bombers and fighter planes would stand ready to cross the Channel and begin their assault on England. Their plan was to smash England's air bases before the German army invaded on land. The Battle of Britain — the summer and fall of dogfights over England, and the devastating bombing of London — would soon begin.

The RAF's Fighter Command knew the odds were against them — their small force was outnumbered three to one. They had to build more planes fast, and they desperately needed pilots to fly them. The RAF agreed to give Bader another chance. He'd have to take a refresher course and pass a test.

As Bader reported to the airfield, he realized it had been over seven years since he'd flown an airplane. Aircraft had changed — a lot. He would be rusty, there was no doubt. For a moment, his confidence flagged. What if I fail? He put the thought out of his mind.

At the end of the course Bader had a chance to read his report. His eyes scanned the page. There was the heading he was looking for: "Ability as a pilot." Under it was scrawled, "Exceptional."

Legs or no legs, they'd have to take him back.

In the air once again, Bader was rapidly promoted — from flying officer to flight lieutenant to squadron leader in four months. And the skeptical pilots he was about to lead were in for a surprise.

The moment Bader arrived at the airfield as the new commander of 242 Squadron, he strode energetically toward one of the Hurricane fighter planes squatting on the runway. No cane, the pilots noticed. In fact, it was hard to tell that this dynamo, full of restless energy, had two metal legs. The only clue was the lurch in his stride as he threw his right leg forward, cracking it like a whip to bend the steel knee and straighten it out again. Bader pulled himself up on the wing and, swinging his leg over the side of the plane, settled into the cockpit.

For half an hour he put the Hurricane through its paces over the airfield, as the pilots stood watching from below. Three loops in a row, then straight ahead in a spin. Climbing up for a final loop, the Hurricane began to spin at the top, then came out of the spin and finished the loop. After a neat landing, Bader hauled himself out without help and marched briskly past the pilots, who stood openmouthed and speechless.

The squadron was a battle-weary group of Canadians, who'd been let down by commanders before. It wasn't long before Bader won them over. He had a temper and could be gruff. But he seemed fearless, and his confidence was contagious.

In the brief lull before the battle he knew was coming — after the fall of France but before Germany launched its assault on Britain — Bader took his squadron through grueling sessions in the air, testing their skills with loops and spins, all in tight formation. He knew the pilots must not be afraid to push themselves and their aircraft to the limit. They must be able to lock onto the tail of an enemy plane and never be shaken off, no matter how wildly it maneuvered to escape.

Never forget, Bader would tell them, he who gets in close shoots them down.

And when the calls started coming from the Operations Room — enemy aircraft sighted, all pilots "scramble!" — they were ready.

★ ★ ★

Now, a year after the Luftwaffe's first savage air strikes, the Spitfires kept climbing as they crossed the Channel. They flew in "finger four" formation, the planes in each group of four spread out like four fingers on an outstretched right hand. Leading his pack of four, Bader was easy to recognize by the large "DB" on the side of his camouflage-colored Spitfire. Bader had painted it there so his men could spot him. A cheeky pilot had jokingly asked if it stood for "Dogsbody," and the name had stuck. Now it was Bader's call sign.

The sun's glare pierced the cockpit glass. Bader's eyes were already burning under his goggles, his body sweating. But that was the least of his worries, he realized. He knew the sun hid their enemies, the Germans' silver-colored fighter planes — Messerschmitt 109s.

That much had not changed since World War I, when dog-fighters such as Billy Bishop had warned, "Beware the Hun in the sun." It was the enemy's favorite direction for attack, coming out of the sun, their prey blinded by the glare.

Now, high above the French coast, Bader rolled his head from side to side, scanning the sky for the dark outlines of enemy planes. Glancing down through the broken clouds he glimpsed bursts of fire from the Germans' anti-aircraft guns, then the patchwork of farmers' fields.

In his mind Bader quickly went over the setbacks so far. It was not one of his best days. First the radio, and then his airspeed indicator. Now one of the squadrons was missing. They were sup-posed to fly above Bader's group, covering them. They must have gone astray.

A voice crackled over the radio. "Dogsbody, 109s below, climbing up."

"Where are they? I can't see them." Bader's tone was crisp.

"Under your port wing."

There! Ahead, to the left, he could see a dozen Messerschmitt

109s. They were flying about 2,000 feet below the Spitfires, climbing slowly and turning toward them.

Perfect, he thought. A climbing aircraft is a sitting duck for an attack — it's moving slowly and is hard to maneuver. As Bader well knew, the pilot flying the highest controls the battle. The advantage was definitely theirs.

"Dogsbody attacking." Leading his group of four, Bader dove. Too fast! He had misjudged and was now hurtling toward one of the enemy planes much too steeply.

There was no time to fire. Bader swerved and dove under the 109, barely missing it. Plunging far below the battle, he finally leveled out at 24,000 feet and looked around. Nothing but blue sky. He was alone.

Bader cursed his bad judgment. He was too tense. He hadn't flown so rashly since the first time he'd seen an enemy plane. Now he knew better: it was useless to rush at the enemy like that. Always approach the target slowly. You'll never get him in a hurry. Maybe his exhaustion was showing — he'd been flying missions almost daily for five months.

But what now? He could continue toward the mission target and hope to link up with the others. Or he could follow the advice he gave his pilots when they found themselves alone — dive to ground level and go home. It was too dangerous to be on your own in a hostile sky.

Then a sight up ahead took him by surprise. Three pairs of Messerschmitt 109s flying with their tails to him. He knew where they were headed — for the British bombers.

Bader dropped below and patiently closed the distance between them. If they see me, he thought, I'll dive and return to base. No 109 can keep up with a Spitfire in a dive.

But they didn't see him. His own words to his pilots surfaced again in his mind — Don't try to fight alone. But he couldn't let them reach the target! He looked behind him — there was no one on his tail.

Ignoring his own advice, Bader closed in on the middle pair and fired. The rear 109 plunged down, streaming flames and white smoke. The other planes kept flying. Bader was surprised. Were they blind?

Bader couldn't resist the temptation to take one more shot. He quickly closed in on the plane still in the middle, steadying his Spitfire in the 109's rough slipstream. Then, lining it up in his sights, he opened fire.

His thumb was still pressed against the fire button when he suddenly glimpsed the two planes on his left turning their yellow noses toward him. In seconds he would be trapped.

Bader shot a glance at the pair of 109s on his right. They were still flying straight ahead, the sunlight shimmering on their silver bodies, the black crosses visible on their sides. He knew that with their guns fixed to fire ahead they were harmless to him, unless they turned. I'll pass over them, he thought, then dive and head home.

Bader banked sharply to the right. The next instant he felt a jolt behind the cockpit. Out of the corner of his eye he saw the tail of a 109 pass behind him.

Then he had the strangest feeling — as if something had grabbed the tail of his plane and pulled it out of his control. The nose of his Spitfire plunged downward. Bader quickly pulled back on the control column to right it. Nothing happened. The stick moved loosely backward in his hand. He looked behind him, and the sight sent his mind reeling.

There was nothing behind the cockpit. The body, the tail of his Spitfire — all gone. The 109 must have hit me, he thought. Sliced me in half with its propeller. But it all seemed so unreal.

Out of habit he glanced at the controls. The altimeter's needle was spinning fast — he had already fallen 4,000 feet. The broken airspeed indicator was still stuck at zero. Never mind that now. Bader was well aware he was hurtling toward the earth in a terrifying spiral.

He forced back a surge of panic. Then, as he plunged earthward, he was amazed at how clear, how detached his mind was. In the seconds that followed, one thought filled his head. He had to get out. Now.

He tore off his oxygen mask. Reaching above his head he pulled the rubber ball suspended there. The transparent hood over the cockpit tore off and flew away.

Bader was in the open now, and the noise was deafening. The wind roared around him as he spiraled downward in the open cockpit, strapped tightly in his harness.

I'm moving too fast... I'm in the wrong position. What if I can't push myself out with only my arms? Bader struggled to focus his mind as the wind howled and buffeted him.

Held fast by his harness, Bader found he could still move his hands. He fumbled with the harness pin and unfastened it.

Right away he felt as if he were being sucked out by a giant vacuum. The wind tore his helmet and goggles off his head. His body began to rise out of the cockpit. Almost out!

And then he stopped.

Something was holding him, he thought wildly, holding onto his right leg. He struggled uselessly. His right foot was caught — hooked under something. What?

The battered Spitfire continued its plunge, pulling Bader with it. As he writhed to free himself, a great pounding noise filled his

head. In his right hand he gripped the parachute release ring, and vaguely he remembered that he must hang on.

Time seemed to slow down. The noise and speed made any more thinking impossible as Bader twisted and pulled on his trapped leg.

Then, with a snap, the leather and steel belt that held his metal leg to his body burst under the strain. Bader had the strange feeling of falling upwards. He was free. The hammering noise stopped, and Bader closed his eyes. Then with a jolt his mind focused again.

The parachute release!

Bader pulled the ring. The parachute spread open above him, and now he was floating in the sunlight. Below he could see white clouds. I must be at about 4,000 feet, he thought. Just in time. A Messerschmitt 109 buzzed past, but left him alone.

Bader looked down at his flapping pant leg and saw that his right leg was gone. And suddenly it occurred to him: If my leg had been real I'd have gone down with the plane. For the first time he felt lucky to have detachable legs.

Once he was through the clouds he could see the farms of northern France below. Drifting gently, he watched a man in a cap carrying a yoke on his shoulders, and a woman with a scarf over her head. They were opening a gate between two fields when they looked up and spotted him. They froze and stared.

I must look pretty odd, Bader thought. Floating down with no leg.

A quiet feeling of peace, of freedom crept over him. He knew the calm was an illusion. Later would come the shock of landing, when the ground rushed up at him and he crashed down inside enemy territory.

But for now, after the chaos of the hour he'd survived, he gave himself over to this strange feeling of silently floating toward earth.

★ ★ ★

Douglas Bader was found by German soldiers who took him to a hospital to recover before continuing on to a prisoner of war camp. He soon learned that the Germans had heard of him, and were amazed that the RAF would let a legless man fly. They were so impressed by his determination that they even let him sit in the cockpit of a Messerschmitt 109! For a few seconds Bader toyed with the idea of taking off, but a German officer kept his pistol aimed squarely at him the whole time. Bader did convince his captors to retrieve his leg from the crash site and mend it, as well as radio England with a request for a new one. He secretly hoped that call would let everyone at home know he was still alive.

At the hospital, a sympathetic nurse smuggled a note to him from the French Resistance — the underground network of men and women working in secret against the Germans who occupied their country. The Resistance would hide Bader if he could find a way out. He escaped out of the hospital window with a rope made from knotted bed sheets, and followed his French contact through the dark to a farmhouse.

A German search party soon banged on the door. Bader slipped out to the barn and hid under the hay, lying still as the soldiers searched the barn. Then, to his horror, he glimpsed the steel of a bayonet piercing through the hay, moving closer with each stroke. When it struck his sleeve, Bader knew there was only one thing he could do. He jumped to his feet before the next stroke could hit home, his arms in the air.

Bader's new leg did arrive — dropped by parachute from an English bomber. But his German captors were so worried he would try another escape on the way to the camp that they took both his legs away for the trip! Bader spent the rest of the war as a prisoner in Germany. But he never stopped trying to escape.

When Douglas Bader returned home after the war, he was asked to lead 300 RAF planes in a special victory fly-past over London, to commemorate the country's triumph in the Battle of Britain. Londoners filled the streets to watch the sky darken once again — not with enemy bombers this time, but with their own beloved Spitfires and Hurricanes.

Under Siege

Oxford, England, 1142

THE DISTANT POUNDING STOPPED. The hail of stones on the castle's curtain wall had slowed and then ended suddenly. The king's great catapults and army of slingers had withdrawn — for the moment at least. Deep within the castle walls, knights and foot soldiers paused at the sudden silence. A sense of relief swept through the garrison. They knew it would not last long, and archers scrambled to prepare for the next assault.

Above them high in the keep, their lady, the Empress Matilda, pulled her robes closer around her and paced the floor to keep warm. The December wind seemed to pierce the stone walls, despite the heavy tapestries that blanketed them, and the fire in the great hearth could not be built up any further. Every piece of wood was precious now.

For nearly three months she and her followers had lived as prisoners within her own castle, surrounded by King Stephen's army, deafened by the battering of his siege engines. Looking around the crowded garrison quarters, she had seen the hunger in her men's gaunt faces, the growing panic in their eyes. And now the castle's great well was nearly dry. Where were her allies? They must come soon to break the blockade. If they didn't...

Matilda pushed the thought from her mind with a defiant toss of her head. Peering sideways through a narrow window, she could see Stephen's flags, the glint of his men's armor in the winter sun.

Anger flared inside her. Who was he to call himself King of England? She had the stronger claim — the only claim — to the throne. She was the daughter of the late King Henry. Stephen was only his nephew. Her father had made all the powerful men of the country swear an oath of loyalty to her, and promise to recognize her as their next queen.

King Henry had still hoped for a male heir — a grandson was his last chance. And so Matilda became a pawn in her father's search for a powerful alliance. At twelve she was married to a German emperor in his thirties. After his death she was betrothed to the thirteen-year-old son of the French Count of Anjou. When at last her father recalled her to England, she had lived away longer than she had ever been at home. As she listened to the barons' oaths, she realized her country had become a land of strangers to her.

And where were those loyal barons now? When her father died, Matilda had been away in France, expecting a child. The barons who had never liked the idea of a woman ruling England jumped upon the chance. At their urging, her young cousin Stephen seized the crown.

And now to be trapped like this! She bristled at the thought.

Then she smiled bitterly — they wouldn't have a woman, but look at the state of the country under Stephen! These were lawless, dangerous times. Barons declared their loyalty to the king, but it was mere words. They raided the countryside, seized lands, took what they liked, and then retreated into their castles.

Stephen may have acted boldly when he snatched the crown, Matilda mused, but he was too mild-mannered, too forgiving to keep the barons in line. When Stephen did not punish them, they smelled weakness.

It had been easy to lure many of the barons back to her side when she sailed to England to challenge Stephen. But she knew they would switch sides again when it suited them. They would be watching for any sign that she or Stephen was gaining the upper hand. No one wanted to be caught on the losing side — and their new leader would be certain to reward their loyalty generously.

Matilda's eyes shone with defiance as she watched the royal troops outside. Whatever happened, she told herself, she must never show weakness.

★ ★ ★

Beyond the castle's curtain wall, across the wide moat, the king's army was a hive of activity. For weeks, the noise of hammering had filled the air as carpenters built a siege tower to soar into the sky. From it Stephen's men would be able to spy on the garrison inside the castle.

Further back other men were repairing a shed on wheels. Under its cover, miners would crawl close to the walls and dig under the stone, hoping to weaken the wall and bring it crashing down. Here and there assaults were being planned, as teams with crossbows or slingshots prepared to storm the castle walls.

And in the midst of it all sat Stephen, on horseback, watching. His gaze now and then returned to one of the castle walls rising out of a huge mound of stone and earth, and the massive ten-sided stone tower that stretched high before him.

A weary sigh escaped his lips. The castles of England, once built to help the king impose his rule across the land, were now being used against him. The kings before him had laid down two rules — no baron could build a castle without the king's permission, and the castle's keys must be surrendered when asked for in the king's name.

Now Stephen's barons sneered at these rules. Ever since Matilda's ship had brought her back to England's shores, she had given the rebel barons a cause around which to rally. She egged on their treachery, urging them to fortify castles to stand against the royal army.

Stephen bitterly remembered the day when at last, like a man shaken from sleep, he had been roused to anger. But was he too late? By then nearly all of southwestern England had fallen into Matilda's hands, her knights controlling a strong belt of castles that stretched from the port of Bristol to her headquarters at Oxford.

After raising an army of loyal subjects in the north, Stephen had begun a grim march — laying siege to Matilda's castles along the way. Some garrisons he had terrified into surrender. Others he had found empty, the soldiers having fled when they heard he was coming. These Stephen burned. Castle by castle, the royal army closed in on Matilda's stronghold at Oxford, cutting her off from her helpers.

Near the end of September, as the feast of Michaelmas approached, Stephen's army had paused before the Thames River. At the head of his troops, Stephen gazed across the water at the city of Oxford. It was well protected by the deep river. To one side a timber palisade guarded the city; on the other rose its castle and soaring tower.

Stephen hadn't waited for long before the enemy showed itself. They came running out of the city gates, toward the Thames. Some shouted insults across the river, others shot arrows over the water. With the river lying between them and the invaders, Matilda's troops felt invincible.

Stephen had seethed with rage. He turned to his advisers. Was there no way across?

One showed him the shallowest point of the river, but warned that even it was very deep.

Stephen wasted no time. He boldly plunged in, leading his men into the deep water. The army waded across, then swam when the water rose over their heads. Their heavy chain mail dragged them down as they struggled to hold their flags above the water.

Streaming up the opposite bank, they charged. Matilda's men were quickly overwhelmed, and ran back through the city gates.

Stephen's troops followed in hot pursuit, pouring through the gates in a fierce column. Once inside, they spread through the streets, throwing firebrands among the houses, capturing as many of Matilda's followers as they could find. Their new prisoners were put in chains — they could be traded for a ransom later.

The rest of Matilda's force fled with their lady in a desperate retreat to the castle, where they shut themselves inside. And left Stephen with no choice but to do this the hard way.

★ ★ ★

Once the heavy doors closed behind her, Matilda had felt safe in her stronghold. Inside the high stone keep, she was confident she could withstand anything Stephen brought against her. She knew the three enemies of people under siege — hunger, thirst, and fire. Her castle had ample supplies and a deep well, and its towering stone walls would not burn.

Let him come, she thought. And her knights braced themselves for the assault.

They did not have to wait long. First a rain of stones slung against the walls, then showers of arrows from a host of crossbows. Stephen's methods were simple: surround the castle and bombard it nonstop.

Matilda's knights fought back. They rained down stones and quicklime on the attackers from the top of the castle, and aimed their bows through the arrow-loops that slit the stone walls. They kept a strict watch for any scouts or assault teams who might try to crawl up the mound at the castle's base. And they waited anxiously for the siege engines they knew the King could bring to batter the castle defenses. Monstrous catapults that hurled rocks into or over the walls. Battering rams to break down the doors.

While her men held the king's army at bay, Matilda plotted her next move. She could take her time. She knew sieges moved slowly — weeks, months could pass with both sides in a standoff. There was plenty of time for reinforcements to arrive. Time for her half-brother, Earl Robert, or her husband to come to her aid. Months ago, Robert had sailed to France to convince Matilda's husband, Geoffrey of Anjou, to join her cause. But she had heard nothing since. Where were they?

Robert was always one to play for time, Matilda reasoned. He'd wait for the right moment. But deep down she knew that any help from her husband was doubtful. They were not close. Still, he might act for their son's sake, if not hers — to protect young Henry's birthright in England!

Just hold out, she told herself. Help is on the way.

★ ★ ★

Stephen knew that laying siege to Matilda and her knights would be a long, ugly struggle. Matilda was no fool and had surely stocked the castle well with food and supplies. But Stephen had already learned that as long as she was on the loose he would have no peace. It seemed he had spent most of his reign dashing from castle to castle, laying siege to rebel after rebel. No sooner was one rebel army defeated than another reared its head, defying him to attack. This time he would not budge.

Messengers arrived, breathless with news. Matilda's allies had joined their forces about 15 miles down the Thames at Wallingford. Then word came that Earl Robert had returned from France and attacked Stephen's garrison at Wareham. The royal troops inside the castle were "shaken and terrified by the Earl's siege engines," they said. The castellan had asked Robert for a truce so he could summon help from the king.

But Stephen refused to be lured away from the Oxford siege. "No hope of gain, no fear of loss will make me go away," he declared, "unless the castle is surrendered and the empress brought into my power."

Nothing would drag him from his goal — to capture Matilda and end the war.

★ ★ ★

Staring at the dying embers of her small fire, Matilda could no longer ignore the doubts that plagued her mind. The siege had entered its third grueling month. Winter deepened.

She and her knights were famished. Scarcely eating, they tried to make their meager supplies last as long as possible. When the well dried up, they drank wine. Now that was nearly gone.

Day by day, Matilda's fears had mounted. Now she was certain. No help was coming. And outside, an army of more than a thousand enemy knights surrounded the castle, battering it with stones. It was only a matter of time now before her garrison would be forced to surrender.

Unconditional surrender. It was an outcome Matilda had never dreamed of. Now she imagined the long line of defeated knights streaming from the castle, Stephen's trumpets sounding in victory. And she pictured the part that tradition held for her — to walk out barefoot and in tears, her hair loose around her shoulders, begging Stephen for her very life.

No, she thought, rising and crossing the room. She was too proud to play that role. She must escape, before the walls crumbled and the starved garrison fell to the King. But how?

Stephen had posted guards all around the castle walls, with orders to keep a strict watch day and night. No one must be allowed to sneak out. How could she get past his watchmen? And even if she could, the whole of Stephen's army lay around the castle, his soldiers blocking every route.

Matilda gazed at the frozen landscape outside. Icy winds swept over deep snow as far as the eye could see. And where would she go in that wasteland? Why, it was so cold this year the Thames was frozen solid!

She drew in sharp breath as a sudden idea came to her. Perhaps the harsh winter could be a friend as well as a foe. But she would need help. In her mind she cast over the knights in her service. She would need to choose carefully — she wanted men who were wary, sensible, and absolutely loyal. No hotheads! Yes, three knights came to mind. She would speak to them at once. Alone.

★ ★ ★

In the stillness of a pitch-dark night, just before Christmas, Stephen's sentries paced at the foot of the castle walls, blowing on their frozen hands, stamping their feet to keep warm. High above their heads, a rope snaked its way out of a tower window, down the steep wall toward the ground.

Unseen by the guards below, Matilda clung to the rope as it was lowered down the sheer wall. The wind lashed at her face and made her white garments flap. Suddenly her descent halted and for a nerve-wracking instant she just hung there, swaying. She squeezed her eyes shut and tightened her grip.

Then she felt herself drop again. Willing her eyes open, she forced herself to look down. Below, one of her trusted knights was waiting for her. In his white clothes, she could hardly make him out against the snow. Good, she thought, their camouflage was working.

The wind picked up, and sharp, wet snow stung her cheeks. But she didn't mind. She knew a snowstorm would make it hard to see your hand in front of your face. It could be the stroke of luck they needed!

Below, one of her accomplices held up his arms to guide her to the ground. When Matilda had first proposed this scheme, the knights had wondered if the hunger had gone to her head! Walking out through Stephen's troops, dressed in white so they would disappear against the snow? It was madness! But Matilda was determined. Her subjects were familiar with her fierce will. Once her mind was made up there was no changing it.

Above Matilda, the last of her escape party was inching his way down. As soon as he touched the ground, the four of them set out cautiously across the snow, toward the royal troops whose camps lay in every direction.

Silently they tiptoed forward, threading their way through the sleeping army. No one stirred. Moving slowly through the blowing snow, Matilda and her knights circled around the tents of sleeping soldiers and little pockets of watchmen.

Matilda fought the urge to run, to dash through the encampment and be off! But she did not dare quicken her careful pace. She could barely see a few steps ahead in the storm. It would be too easy to stumble on an enemy foot or leg in the darkness. One false step would be their undoing.

Then, out of the corner of her eye, Matilda spotted a sudden movement. She froze and signaled to her knights to stop in their tracks. A figure was moving toward them through the darkness. Matilda prayed they would be invisible through the swirling snow. As the figure drew closer, she could see it was a sentry. But could he see them?

The sentry peered through the darkness, his eyes scanning back and forth in their direction. Matilda stood frozen in place, not daring to speak or move. The sentry blinked as if to clear his eyes, then started walking straight toward her.

The knight at her side silently crouched down and began to creep in a circle around the approaching soldier. As the sentry came closer, his eyes widened — he had seen them! He opened his mouth to shout, but a firm hand clapped over it. While the knight held him from behind, Matilda and her two companions moved swiftly forward.

Making a silent plea with her eyes, Matilda slipped a fistful of coins into the sentry's palm, and placed her finger to her lips. He blinked and nodded slightly.

The white-clad group moved on, faster now. Matilda could feel the wind pick up, and she knew the icy expanse of the Thames lay ahead. They were almost at the riverbank. A moment later Matilda placed a wary foot on the ice, and then her whole weight. It's solid, she thought with relief. She and her knights spread out and crept forward cautiously, testing the ice with each step.

Behind them the silence of the night was suddenly broken by loud shouts and blaring trumpets. Curse him, Matilda thought, the sentry must have raised the alarm! She pressed ahead as quickly as she dared. The wind swept around her as she moved across the frozen water, and she felt keenly how exposed she was — out in the open for everyone to see!

Or perhaps not, Matilda reminded herself. Her only hope was that their white clothes were once again hiding them from their pursuers. Without a backward glance, she kept going, struggling to keep her footing on the ice.

With a surge of relief, Matilda stepped onto the opposite bank. The clamor of enemy soldiers sounded distant now. How remarkable, she thought suddenly. To think I have crossed with dry feet, without wetting any of my garments, the very waters into which the king and his troops plunged up to the neck!

But her odyssey was far from over. Six miles of frozen countryside lay between her and her nearest friends. The four escapers trudged close together for fear of getting lost in the blizzard — through snow and ice, down steep ditches and up treacherous hills. Exhausted and frozen, they stumbled toward Abingdon, where supporters of Matilda's cause gave them horses.

They did not dare rest at Abingdon for long. Mounting their horses, the group galloped to Matilda's stronghold at Wallingford, where her allies welcomed her with astonished joy.

When Earl Robert heard of Matilda's daring escape he rushed to join her. He had been at Cirencester, trying to rally an army of supporters to march to her aid at Oxford. Upon Robert's arrival Matilda sprang forward to greet him, but was stopped in her tracks by the odd smile that played on her brother's features. As he stepped to one side, she saw what he had been hiding behind his back — her nine-year old son, Henry, brought with him from France. No other sight could have so restored Matilda's hopes. As she wrapped her arms around him, the past months seemed to slip away, forgotten.

★ ★ ★

Once Matilda's getaway was assured, her garrison at Oxford surrendered to Stephen's army. Stephen stayed a while in Oxford, bringing that rebellious part of the country under his control at last. And the townspeople and peasants of the ravaged countryside — always the first to suffer hunger and loss during a siege — began to piece their lives back together.

The chroniclers of the Middle Ages marveled at Matilda's cunning. One wrote, "Certainly I have never heard of any woman having such marvelous escapes from so many enemies threatening her life, and from such exceeding perils." But for all her cleverness, Matilda was never able to take the throne back from Stephen. In time she was rewarded, though — when her son became King Henry II.

The Gladiator War

Capua, Italy, 73 B.C.

THE YOUNG THRACIAN LIFTED HIS SWORD to ward off the blow. Then another. Sweating now, he dodged around his larger, heavily armed opponent, looking for an opening to make a thrust with his own weapon. The combat was fierce, and the midday sun beat mercilessly upon the two men. Then, lunging desperately forward, the Thracian opened himself to attack. Quickly he swiveled behind his small shield, but it was too late — with a forceful blow his opponent's sword fell across his bare chest.

Panting, the young man stopped and looked down to where the weapon pressed against his skin, but drew no blood. In the heat of the contest, he'd almost forgotten — the sword was wooden.

But in the arena it will be real, he thought, as he let his own wooden blade and shield fall to his side. And I won't get off so easily then.

Standing nearby, his trainer shook his head and spit into the sand. It was his job to turn the slaves assigned to him into gladiators — men who fought each other with weapons in public spectacles. The young man's name was Spartacus, but to his trainers he was just another slave, like the rest of the outcasts who crowded the barracks of the *ludi,* or gladiatorial school.

To Spartacus, it seemed like a lifetime since he was captured by the Roman army in his homeland of Thrace, a land of nomadic shepherds. Bound in chains, he had been taken over sea and land to Rome, to be sold as a slave. Seeing that he was young and strong, his captors forced him to serve in the Roman army for a time, before selling him to be trained as a gladiator.

His story was a common one. As the Roman army conquered the lands around the Mediterranean Sea, more and more prisoners were shipped back to Italy to work as slaves for wealthy Romans. The Roman Republic's demand for new slaves seemed endless — they needed them to farm their huge tracts of land, to shepherd their flocks, to work in their dangerous mines, to entertain them.

And Roman taste in entertainment ran to the spectacular — and the violent. In a warrior state such as theirs, martial skill and courage were highly prized. The strongest and healthiest of the slaves might be bought by a *lanista,* a man who owned and trained gladiators — "men of the sword." In giant amphitheaters these trained fighters would engage in armed combat for the entertainment of crowds, and the honor of the powerful men who paid for the spectacle.

For even more variety and excitement, gladiators with different fighting styles and armor would be pitted against each other. A lightly armed *retiarius,* holding a trident and a net to entangle his opponent, might face off against a slower, armored *secutor,* whose helmet and large shield offered some protection from the *retiarius's* three-pronged spear.

The rituals of the arena may have been dramatic, but there was nothing staged about the fighting. Contests were often fought to the death. The defeated gladiator's only hope was to appeal to the crowd and the patron of the games for a *missio,* a decision to let him live. But this was granted only if he had fought bravely enough to capture the spectators' sympathy. And they were not easy to impress.

For while the Roman crowds adored the performances, at the same time they held the gladiators in contempt. These fighters were the dregs of society, only slightly better than *bestiarii,* the slaves trained to fight wild animals.

Of course the Romans knew enough to keep a close guard on these men they had trained for combat but doomed to slavery. In the barracks that circled the *ludi's* sandy training yard, the fighters were locked in cells at night, their weapons secured in an armory well away from them.

Still, the Romans weren't unduly alarmed. Everyone knew Rome's army was all-powerful. And these slaves — riffraff from Gaul, Germany, Thrace, Syria. They couldn't be much of a threat.

No one seemed to realize just how desperate Spartacus and men like him were. What could he hope for at the end of his harsh training? After the discipline and punishments of the school barracks, with its stocks and chains? A banquet the night before the gladiatorial games. A few hours before the cheering crowds. What then? Some of his fellow slaves clung to the hope of winning their freedom — they'd heard stories of a few talented fighters who'd been set free. Or maybe they'd survive long enough to become trainers themselves.

But Spartacus knew the chances of that were slim at best. Most gladiators could hope to fight two, maybe three times in the arena before being killed. It wouldn't be long now before he was riding in a cart, on the way to his first combat. His first and perhaps his last. Yet what choice did he have?

Master and slave. It was the way things were, and always would be.

Wouldn't they?

In the days and months ahead, Spartacus would shatter this idea, and others the Romans held dear, forever.

★ ★ ★

Word quickly spread through the cramped barracks: There's going to be a breakout. Will you come? More and more of the desperate gladiators agreed, until 200 men were in on the secret.

It was the height of summer in the rich city of Capua in southern Italy, the center for gladiator training. For weeks, Spartacus had eyed the gladiators around him, sizing up these men from far-off countries — Thracians like himself, as well as Gauls, Germans, and Syrians. Some were slaves, some condemned criminals, others prisoners of war. But many of them were free-born, and still carried the memory of freedom. It had been easy to convince them to act.

Their scheme was bold and simple: to gather in the training yard, slowly, without raising suspicion. There they would grab the training weapons at hand and rush the guards. With luck they'd overpower them by their sheer numbers. Beyond that they had no plan, and no idea what would be waiting outside for them. For now, getting out was all that mattered.

But on the humid summer evening before the escape, terrible news reached Spartacus: someone had talked. Their master and *lanista,* Lentulus Batiatus, knew of the plan and who the ringleaders were. A local militia was on its way to make an example of the would-be escapers. The gladiators looked at one another helplessly. What could they do?

"We go now," Spartacus replied firmly, "before the guards lock us in for the night." He knew they still had a chance if they acted swiftly.

Over half the plotters slunk away to their cells, fearing it would be crazy to plunge ahead now that the plan had been discovered. Those left behind quickly weighed their options. Their weapons were locked in the armory, leaving them defenseless.

"Think!" hissed a Gaul named Crixus, keenly aware that armed officials could be on the grounds at any moment. "Is there nothing to defend ourselves with?"

"The kitchen — we can still get in there!" Spartacus cried suddenly. Storming through the barracks, the gladiators burst into the school's kitchen. They grabbed knives, forks, cooking spits — anything sharp that could serve as a weapon.

Armed now, they streamed out of the kitchen into the moonlit training yard. Barely slowing down, Spartacus stooped to pick up a handful of stones, and hurled them at the startled guards. With cries and shouts the other gladiators followed his example, and the guards raised their arms to shield themselves. In that instant the gladiators rushed upon them with their knives and spits.

In minutes they had broken out of the school and flooded onto the streets of Capua, their hearts pounding.

"Look!" Crixus cried, breathless.

The gladiators stopped in their tracks, openmouthed. Spartacus couldn't believe their luck. Before them were two wagons loaded with gladiatorial weapons, destined for a contest in another city! Seeing the gladiators, the drivers quickly jumped off the carts and ran. The escaped men eagerly snatched up swords and shields and armed themselves.

About 70 gladiators had made it out. Now they'd need a plan if they were to have a chance of staying free. They chose their leaders on the spot. Two Gauls, Crixus and another man named Oenomaus, were quickly voted captains. But the overwhelming choice for commander was Spartacus. It was obvious to all that the Thracian had the brains and the courage to help them survive. What was more, Spartacus had a special insight into the enemy, having fought in their ranks. That could prove to be a valuable weapon.

But first, the new leaders agreed, they must get out of Capua.

Suddenly, distant shouts and the sound of running feet made Spartacus look up. From all directions, armed citizens were running down the city streets. In moments the escapers would be cornered.

Their backs to the wall, the gladiators clenched their swords and braced themselves for the attack. But in the fierce struggle that followed, the locals were no match for men trained to fight and desperate to stay free. The gladiators quickly overpowered and disarmed them.

Spartacus picked up a Roman weapon and balanced its weight in his hand. With his other hand he threw down the gladiator's sword he'd been holding, as did the others. Barbaric object, he thought. Tainted with dishonor. He'd never touch one again.

★ ★ ★

In Rome, the senators listened impatiently to the messenger's story of gladiators breaking out of a school in Capua. Let the local forces take care of it, they sniffed. Then word came that the rebels had left the city. A slave named Spartacus had led his followers up the treacherous mountain path to the very top of Mount Vesuvius. The gladiators had set up a camp in the volcano's crater. Worse, other runaway slaves were joining them daily, and their growing numbers posed a risk to the region.

Very well, the Roman authorities sighed. They would send a Roman commander. Not a consul — it would be beneath his

dignity— but a praetor, a lesser official. They'd draft a force of 3,000 men to put under his command. That kind of muscle would surely put a quick end to the revolt, the senate reasoned. There was no need to use Rome's highly trained regular army. They were dealing with *slaves,* after all.

In a confident and boastful mood, the newly drafted troops marched swiftly south to the foot of Vesuvius. There they prepared to surround and lay siege to the rebel slaves.

High above, Spartacus and his scouts peered over the tangle

of wild vines that covered the mountaintop, and watched grimly as the Roman army gathered in numbers far below. Roman guards were taking up their posts along the narrow road up the mountain — the only route down. All the other sides of the mountain were as steep and smooth as cliffs.

"They're trapping us," the scouts muttered. "We'll starve up here."

Spartacus was silent for a moment. "If it comes to that," he said at last, "I'd rather die by steel than perish by hunger."

Without another word he crept back from the edge and turned toward the camp in the crater. He wasn't going to give in so easily. Glancing up, he noticed the sun was already high in the sky. There was much to do before dark.

Spartacus put the gladiators to work until nightfall, ripping out the vines that grew all around them. Carefully they twisted the stems into chains, until they were long enough to snake down the face of the mountain. When darkness came they were ready.

Fastening their ropes to the cliff top, the slaves silently scaled down one of the steep, unguarded mountainsides. Above them, one gladiator stayed behind with the weapons until the last of his companions had reached the foot of the mountain. Then he rapidly tossed down the weapons one by one. When the last weapon hit the ground below, he slithered down the vines himself.

The slaves crept silently around the base of the mountain, circling the sleeping Roman camp from behind. Spartacus and his captains paused, listening in the dark for any sounds of enemy movement. But they heard nothing, only their own breathing. Then, at a signal from Spartacus, the slaves rushed forward in a fierce surprise attack. Overwhelmed and bewildered in the darkness, many of the Roman soldiers fled. Spartacus and his followers seized the camp and plundered it for weapons and supplies.

It was a stunning victory, beyond their hopes. And to the slaves of the surrounding countryside, it was the moment they'd dreamed of. Herdsmen and shepherds from the region ran to join the gladiators, who welcomed them. Spartacus knew how valuable such men could be. Their work made them strong and fast, and they could handle weapons — defending their flocks against wild animals and thieves had taught them that. Then came slaves fleeing from surrounding farms. Many weren't trained to fight, but they put their skill at weaving baskets from branches to good use, making shields for the rebels.

Spartacus quickly organized the newcomers according to their skills. Some were given heavy weapons, some turned into light-armed troops, others were made scouts. This was no longer a band of runaways. They were an army now. And a threat that Rome could no longer ignore.

Burning with shame, the Roman Republic sent another praetor to lead soldiers against Spartacus — with orders to swiftly undo the dishonor of the first one's failure.

The Roman defeats that followed were humiliating. The slave army harried the Romans with sudden attacks, surprising one commander while he was bathing, stealing another commander's horse out from under him! Frightened, Roman soldiers began to desert the army. A few tried to join Spartacus, but he turned them away. All the while Spartacus's army grew, from hundreds to thousands. Now, slaves boldly ran from their masters' homes to join them as they passed. The sight of the gladiator army made two things clear. Escape from slavery was possible, and even the Roman army couldn't force them back!

Rome no longer worried about the indignity of fighting slaves. This was no sordid rebellion. The slave army had swelled to tens of thousands of men and women and was moving freely through southern Italy. The whole Roman way of life — balanced so carefully upon slavery — was at risk of falling to pieces. Now fear spurred the Roman senate to put both of the Republic's consuls in command of two legions of infantry and cavalry, over 10,000 men. This time they would fight as they would against a powerful enemy.

But Spartacus knew better than to take on the full force of the Roman army. Some of his men, thrilled by their victories, clamored to march on Rome itself. Spartacus proposed another goal — they would march north to the Alps, and out of Italy to freedom.

"We'll cross the mountains, and then every one to his own homeland. To Gaul, to Germany... and to Thrace."

★ ★ ★

As the mid-winter of 71 B.C. approached, Spartacus stood on the southernmost tip of Italy and gazed out over the choppy waves. He and his army were camped on the bank of the Strait of Messina. Across the water lay the island of Sicily. He was about as far from the Alps as he could be.

It had been a stormy two years. The march north to the mountains had been slowed by arguments among Spartacus's followers, who had become unruly and hard to control. Many were overconfident, fired up by their freedom and victories, and thought only of sweeping through the cities of Italy for plunder.

"It's not gold and silver we need," Spartacus had warned them, "but iron and copper." Basic material for weapons and survival would keep them alive, not stolen ornaments and jewelry.

Other commanders in the slave army had taken revenge on their Roman prisoners of war, holding gladiatorial games and forcing the Roman prisoners to fight each other. Crixus had even split from Spartacus, taking with him a huge number of German slaves. On their own, Crixus's men had been savagely defeated by the consuls' forces.

Yet the two Roman legions had been powerless to stop the bulk of Spartacus's army, and the slaves kept pushing north. Then, just as freedom had seemed within their reach, a Roman governor of Gaul had moved thousands of his soldiers to block the slaves' escape route through the Alps. Spartacus had been forced to turn back. He led his army south, sticking to remote areas far from the cities.

The defeated Roman consuls had been recalled to Rome in disgrace, and it was revealed that their armies had been stripped of much of their weaponry by the slaves. At last the Roman senate grasped the danger they faced. They quickly named Crassus, a well-born and respected commander, as the general in charge of the war, and placed under his command eight legions of the best trained troops. And if Crassus did not crush the slaves fast enough, the famous commander Pompey would be summoned from Spain to finish the job.

That was the last thing Crassus wanted. Pompey was his rival for power, and he knew that whoever arrived last would take credit for winning the war. Crassus was determined to destroy the slave army before Pompey returned. His first action was to make sure his troops were more afraid of him than of Spartacus, and he harshly punished deserters and any soldiers accused of cowardice. Then he prepared for a massive onslaught against the slaves.

Now, almost two years after the breakout at Capua, Spartacus knew that despite all the victories, his army could not hold out any longer. On reaching the southern shores of Italy, Spartacus had bargained with Cilician pirates to take his men in their ships across the strait to Sicily. He knew that a slave revolt had been crushed on that island only a few years before, and he guessed that the memory of it would still be vivid there. Perhaps he and his followers could rekindle the sparks of rebellion.

The pirates took gifts from Spartacus and promised to return with more ships. But Spartacus waited in vain for them on the seacoast. In the meantime, Crassus had followed him south, and set up camp behind the slave army. There, he began to build a fortified wall lined with sharpened stakes and fronted with a deep ditch.

At first Spartacus laughed at the wall. But not for long. The barrier soon stretched from shore to shore straight across the neck of land that led to the southern tip of Italy. Crassus had trapped Spartacus between his wall and the sea.

But Spartacus had not yet run out of tricks. On a snowy winter night, he ordered his men to begin filling a part of the trench with earth and branches. Before Crassus was aware of what was happening, a third of the slave army had crossed the trench and clambered over the wall, and the rest soon forced their way across. Spartacus hoped that if they moved swiftly east to the port of Brundisium, they might sail from Italy across the Adriatic Sea.

He knew it was their last chance for escape, but by now many of his troops thought too highly of themselves to listen to their commander. Spartacus's strategy of sudden attacks followed by retreat — so successful in the past — now seemed beneath them. They were tired of staying on the defensive, forever on the move.

The slender thread of control Spartacus still held over his army snapped at last. Crassus's legions had been close on their heels for days, as the Roman general hoped to force a battle before Pompey's return. Spotting Crassus's nearby camp, a number of hotheaded slaves rushed to attack the soldiers nearest them. In no time, men from either side were leaping into the fray.

Spartacus watched grimly, and he knew that the decision to attack had been snatched out of his hands. On his reluctant command, the rest of his army wheeled around into battle formation, and Spartacus prepared to face Crassus head-on. Leading his men, he rushed straight for the Roman commander. In the brutal struggle that followed, Spartacus was last seen surrounded and outnumbered, defending himself with his raised shield and sword.

★ ★ ★

In the end, it had taken eight Roman legions — about 44,000 men — and two years to defeat Spartacus and his rebels. Pompey did arrive from Spain and stole the glory for the victory from Crassus by catching the last stragglers of the slave army fleeing the battle. The Romans took a terrible revenge on the slaves who had dared to defy them: 6,000 were executed as a warning to other slaves.

Yet even the Roman and Greek historians of the era, who would have liked to describe Spartacus as a low-life barbarian, were forced to admire his ingenuity and courage. To their shock, 3,000 Roman prisoners of war were found unharmed in Spartacus's camp after the slaves' defeat. And Spartacus had died as they believed a man should, boldly leading his troops in battle. It seemed scarcely believable, but this Thracian slave had behaved almost like — dared they say it — a Roman.

Over the Wall

Pössneck, East Germany, 1978

SOMETHING STRANGE WAS DEFINITELY GOING ON. That's the only conclusion 14-year-old Frank Strelzyk could come to. His parents had been going out a lot at night. And they *never* went out. His dad hated how you had to be careful what you said in public. You couldn't complain about your job or criticize the government without worrying that the person next to you would call the police. At least in my own living room I can speak my mind, his dad would say. So his parents usually stayed at home with Frank, watching West German TV. Until recently, that is.

And it wasn't just the nights out that were odd. His dad was spending hours in the garage with their neighbor, Günter Wetzel. Maybe that wasn't so strange — his dad, an electrician, often repaired things at home for extra money. But he usually loved to show Frank how to fix stuff. Now his workshop was off-limits. What were they doing in there?

One day Frank had snuck into the garage and seen the two men standing in front of something weird — it looked like a big airplane propeller. When they saw Frank they nearly jumped out of their skins. A couple of weeks later he passed the open door and had another peek. Inside, a giant roll of fabric leaned against the wall. His dad and Günter exchanged glances. "It's a tent," his dad said as he closed the door, blocking Frank's view.

Frank had wandered into the kitchen, where his mom was staring out the window, a faraway look in her eyes. She didn't even notice Frank at first.

What's happening? he thought. If something's wrong, why don't they tell me? He could understand if they didn't want to worry his younger brother, Andreas.

But why don't they tell *me?* he wondered helplessly. I'm not a little kid anymore.

★ ★ ★

Peter Strelzyk didn't like hiding things from his son, but he couldn't afford to take chances. Not now, not when they were so close.

It had started over a year ago, but back then it was just a game. A game that helped him forget the long hours he worked with nothing to show for it. A game that made him feel better when he could no longer read the newspapers without throwing them down in disgust. They were full of official lies about how good life was in Communist Germany. No one dared say anything different — the secret police's spies were everywhere. Troublemakers might be arrested in the middle of the night, and their neighbors would never find out what happened to them.

Sometimes Peter gazed across town toward the West. Not many miles away was another world he couldn't go see — because of the long stretch of barbed wire that snaked along the border between Communist East Germany and the democratic West. He'd never felt so trapped as when he visited Berlin and saw the looming concrete wall, first built in 1961, that sliced the city in half. The Communist government said it would safeguard the socialist way of life, but everyone soon discovered its real purpose — to keep people in, not enemies out.

And so he'd started playing a game in his head. If I wanted to get out, how would I do it? He asked his friend Günter what he thought.

"There's just no way out by land," Günter said in his usual slow, thoughtful tone. "The fences along the border are crawling with armed guards — in watchtowers and on the ground. They see everything. And even if you were able to get over the barbed wire, there's the death strip."

Peter nodded. Günter didn't have to explain what he meant: the barren strip of land between the barbed wire fence and the final wall bordering West Germany. It was covered with hidden mines that would explode under the lightest footstep, and trip wires that set off hails of automatic bullets.

"And there's no route by boat," Günter went on. "So that leaves only one way. Air."

"But where would we — I mean, someone — get an airplane, or a helicopter?"

Günter shrugged. They both knew it was impossible, unless you were very rich.

Peter couldn't remember who thought of it first. But one day at lunch, one of the friends nudged the other.

"I've got it — a balloon!"

"What?"

"Why don't we build ourselves a balloon?"

Both men grinned. So it wasn't just a game anymore! They were hooked on the idea from the start. Peter was known for solving problems on the assembly line at work. And there wasn't a car engine or machine that Günter couldn't fix. This would be the challenge of their lives!

But how *would* they build it? Neither of them had any first-hand knowledge of balloons.

"Hot air rises," Peter reasoned. "So we heat the cold air inside a big balloon with some kind of flame. But the flame has to be strong. We need enough heat to push the balloon, the basket, and all of us into the air."

That was about all they knew.

The next morning they stopped off at the People's Library to look for a book that could help them. In the sparse collection they found only two helpful items. And one was an entry in an encyclopedia about the first balloon flight in history — 200 years ago!

Peter wasn't discouraged. "If they could do it then," he whispered to Günter, "we should be able to do it today!"

★ ★ ★

Peter sat at the kitchen table, scrawling calculations on a pad. The balloon would need to carry four adults — Peter and his wife, Doris; Günter and his wife, Petra. Plus four kids — Frank, Andreas, and the Wetzels' two children. Then there was the weight of the basket, the heating system and the balloon itself. All in all, about 1,700 pounds!

Peter's pencil scratched until he arrived at the size of balloon they would need to lift it all. He stared at his results. Their balloon would have to hold as much air as a house — a big one! They'd need a huge amount of fabric.

Where would they buy all it all? Not in Pössneck, that was for sure. Stores were so badly stocked, Doris sometimes lined up for hours for groceries, only to find they were sold out when her turn came.

Peter and Günter drove from city to city. At last they found a roll of brown cotton in a department store.

"How much do you need?" asked the salesperson.

Peter glanced around to see if anyone was listening. He paused, then blurted out, "Eight hundred and eighty yards."

The salesperson's jaw dropped. "We run a camping club," he added hastily. "We need to line our tents."

Peter quickly paid cash with his savings and the two men lugged the rolls of fabric back to the car, shoving them into the trunk and back seat. After dark they drove to Günter's house and carried them up to the Wetzels' bedroom in the attic. They couldn't be too careful — a nosy neighbor might report any odd behavior to the police.

Over the next two days they cut the material into huge triangles and long, narrow rectangles. Günter hunched over Petra's forty-year-old sewing machine, pumping the foot pedal to sew the strips together, while Peter fed him the long pieces of fabric.

Outside the bedroom, Petra blocked the door with a ladder. "We're renovating," she told visitors. Günter put a second doorbell in the attic to warn them if someone came to call. After two weeks of labor, Günter's eyes were bleary and his ankles swollen, but they had their balloon — 50 feet wide and 66 feet long.

Next the men drew the curtains in Günter's workshop on the second floor and set to work on the basket and burner. Peter's welding torch sparked for hours as he pieced together the passenger basket from steel posts and wooden boards. He strung a clothesline between the posts for a guardrail.

The gas burner was trickier. It would have to be powerful. Peter rigged two propane bottles to a stovepipe, and prayed they would work.

The two men worked fiendishly, and within a few weeks it was time for a test. Peter and Günter drove around, looking for a place to try out the balloon in secret. Outside town they found a clearing in a wood of tall pine trees. Perfect!

Just before midnight, Peter and Günter stuffed the rolled-up balloon and equipment into the trunk and back seat of the car. Peter could hardly contain his excitement as they drove to the test site and quickly set up.

The burner shot out a flame, but the balloon stayed flat as a pancake. The fabric wasn't airtight! Peter groaned — they'd have to start over.

But they didn't dare buy so much material all at once again — it was too risky. The two men and their wives spread out to hunt for bits and pieces of fabric, driving to different towns and stores to buy airtight taffeta scrap by scrap.

★ ★ ★

On a cool May evening, little more than a month after the first test, the two couples spread their multicolored balloon across the clearing, and Peter started up the blower. The roar was deafening, even with the muffler Peter had added. Günter cringed at the noise.

"Don't worry," Peter shouted in Günter's ear. "People will think it's a motorcycle."

Günter, Doris, and Petra held up the neck of the balloon. Watching Peter, they braced themselves for the impact. Günter nodded, and Peter turned on the blowtorch and burner. The flame streaked out — higher than they expected. Doris and Petra jumped out of the way. Peter's hair was singed as he held the powerful burner steady.

The fabric on the ground began to stir, rippling as the air streamed through it. Peter stared at it as he gripped the burner. Come on, he thought. This time it *has* to work.

Ever so slowly, the colored stripes began to rise off the ground, snapping in the air. The balloon swelled as it lifted high above their heads.

All four stood with their heads tilted back, mouths open in amazement. It was beautiful! Like a dream, the balloon towered over the trees and swayed against the starry sky. Flushed with their first success, Peter shouted for joy.

It was time to tell Frank, he decided. He had worried that the kids would have a hard time keeping a giant balloon a secret. One little hint to their friends, and the whole plan was finished. Worse, they could be arrested. But now Frank was getting suspicious — it might be more dangerous to leave him guessing any longer.

Back at home, Peter led Frank to the garage, and this time he didn't hide anything from his son. As Frank stared at the deflated balloon, basket, and burner, Peter told him the story of their escape plan. Frank blinked with disbelief, then a slow smile spread across his face. It seemed too good to be true!

"We're almost ready to go," his father added.

★ ★ ★

Peter watched Günter as he wandered restlessly around the garage. He had been quiet tonight, even for Günter. Something was wrong.

Finally Günter spoke up. "Petra's been having bad dreams," he said slowly. "She's more afraid now — that we'll get arrested. That we'll crash."

"That's natural..." Peter began to say.

Günter cut him off. "It's not just Petra who's having doubts. Look, we've filled the balloon, but we still don't have enough lifting power." He looked down, avoiding Peter's eyes. "I'm just not sure that we can do it anymore."

Peter nodded. He turned his face to hide his disappointment. How could he blame them? Günter and Petra would have to risk so much.

"It might be better if we didn't see each other," he said at last. "I don't want the police arresting you and Petra as our accomplices."

There was nothing else to say. The two friends shook hands and Günter walked out into the night.

★ ★ ★

Peter stood in his backyard in the crisp spring air and stared at the propane tanks at his feet. It had been a year since that wonderful night when their balloon had filled the sky. Peter was still struggling alone to solve the puzzle of lifting power.

Peter sighed as he upended another used propane bottle. He turned the tap to empty the last bit of gas. Instantly propane streamed out through the opened tap. The pressure was incredible!

That's it! Peter thought. Turning the bottles upside down increases the pressure! That night he confirmed his theory at the test site — the burner's flame was at least 40 feet long.

Nothing was holding them back now. The Strelzyks waited nervously for the right flying weather — a clear night with a westward wind that would blow them over the border. Frank spent days at school staring out the window at a nearby weathervane. Doris and Peter made a point of taking on long-term projects at work, so no one would suspect they had a sudden departure on their minds.

Then one afternoon at school, Frank didn't hear a word his teacher said. The weathervane outside had been pointing steadily in the right direction for hours. The sky was blue — not a cloud in sight. Tonight would be the night!

Back at home, Doris grabbed the family's identification papers and made sure everyone had warm clothes — they would be soaring thousands of feet up in the cold night air. But they took little else with them. Extra weight would be disastrous.

The hours passed slowly as they waited for dark, then for their neighbors' lights to turn off. Slipping through the garage into the car, Peter told the boys to lie down in the back seat, so no one would see them out late.

The motion of the car soon put Andreas to sleep. But Frank was wide awake, his heart racing. He'd never felt so excited — or nervous.

At the clearing they set up quickly, and Peter made a final equipment check: flashlights, matches, altimeter. He started the blower and the balloon began to fill with cold air. Glancing up at the sky, he frowned. A few clouds drifted across the sky. They hadn't been there when they left. But he wasn't turning back now.

It was time to heat the air. He ignited the blowtorch and held the flame to the neck of the balloon. Frank quickly put the burner together. He watched for his dad's signal, then lit it.

The balloon rose so swiftly they were startled. The lines holding the basket to the fabric stretched to the breaking point.

"Come on," Peter shouted as he turned off the blowtorch and threw it down. The four of them scrambled inside and crouched down on the steel floor. Peter and Frank leaned over the sides and cut the cables holding them to the ground.

Slowly, gently, the basket swayed upward. Peter had not expected it would feel like this — he could hardly tell they were moving at all. Doris and the kids watched the trees below get smaller.

Peter kept his eyes on the gas flame. He mustn't let it touch the fabric, no matter what. He gripped the stovepipe to steady the flame in the center. It was as cold as ice! With a groan Peter remembered that he had left his work gloves lying on the ground. And beside them he had dropped the fire extinguisher!

The balloon kept rising in the darkness. Within minutes they had passed 3,000 feet, then 4,000, and still they soared higher. Peter guessed it would take them half an hour to reach West Germany. How much time had it been so far — 10, 20 minutes? Not long now, he told himself.

Suddenly Peter felt like he'd been drenched in a wet fog. They were in the clouds!

Don't panic, he thought. But he knew the balloon would soak up the water in the clouds like a sponge. It would make them heavier. And slower.

The basket started spinning, buffeted by strong winds. They'd hit turbulence! Peter quickly turned down the gas, and they sank under the clouds.

No one noticed at first that they kept sinking. Peter was blinded by the burner's hot flame. Why didn't I bring goggles? he thought uselessly. But when the others looked over the side, they saw the lights below getting bigger.

Shouts filled the balloon as everyone realized at once — they were going down.

"We're dropping!"

"Look out!"

There was no time to turn up the gas to lift them back up. Before Peter could react, he heard fabric tearing as the balloon sailed through the treetops. Pine branches gripped the balloon as it passed, slowing it down. Before they knew what was happening, they hit the ground.

"Everyone out!" Peter ordered. He didn't know what might

happen — the propane might explode, or the balloon might fall, trapping them.

One by one they hopped over the guardrail and ran into the woods. From a hiding spot they looked around, panting.

Where were they?

Peter's mind raced. They'd been in the air for more than half an hour. Chances were, they'd made it.

"Stay here while I look around," he said.

Peter walked alone out of the woods and spotted a fence up ahead. No, he thought. Two fences, high ones, with a strip between them. He tried to stay calm. Was it the border?

And which side were they on?

Peter returned to the woods. "Follow me," he whispered to his family. "Slowly."

They crept through the dark with the flashlight off, afraid its light would give them away. Peter stumbled on something. He lit the flashlight, shielding the beam with his hand and moved forward.

The light fell across something odd — wires spiraling across their path, about waist high.

Holding the others back, Peter swung his leg carefully over the wires. There were more ahead. He followed the length of one of the wires with the flashlight, and saw where it connected to a box.

Trip wires! Fear gripped Peter's mind. Do the West Germans use trip wires on their side? He didn't know. But they couldn't go any further in the dark, not with these deadly traps threading all around them. The slightest brush against them would set off an alarm — or automatic bullets. They'd have to wait until dawn.

Frank stooped down and picked something up. It was a torn package. Peter aimed his flashlight at it, and as they read the print, their hearts sank: "People's Owned Bakery, Wernigerode."

They were still in East Germany, just short of the border fences. Without speaking, Peter clicked off the flashlight. The four of them huddled together, and waited for first light.

★ ★ ★

If only. Those words haunted Peter when they got back home. If only they hadn't hit the clouds. If only he'd noticed sooner that they were sinking. He could have turned up the flame for the burst of speed they needed to carry them over the border. They were so close! The thought tortured him.

As the days passed, his hands stopped shaking, and he told himself that they had been lucky. A little further and they would have landed in the minefield.

Now something worse weighed on his mind — there was no going back to their old life. They'd left a balloon lying in the border zone. The police would search for the failed escapers. The newspaper had already carried a picture of the things they'd left in the abandoned balloon, asking people to come forward with information about the "crime."

It was only a matter of time before some clue — the fabric they'd bought, a witness who'd seen them driving to the clearing — led the secret police to their door.

There was only one thing to do: build another balloon. Fast. But this time Peter knew they couldn't do it alone.

★ ★ ★

Günter had pricked up his ears when he heard rumors of a torn balloon found near the border. Was it Peter's? He hadn't spoken to his friend since they'd agreed to go their separate ways.

When Peter knocked on his door, he had been surprised. He had listened eagerly to the details of the flight, the old excitement coming back. Peter described what had gone wrong.

"But you should have seen it, Günter! The takeoff and the flight were so smooth." Günter's eyes had grown brighter as he listened.

"If you had been there to navigate, Günter, we would have made it," Peter added. "I know it."

"I'll have to think about it, Peter."

But Günter had already known what his answer would be. Since they had backed out, he and Petra had regretted their decision more and more each day.

Now, standing beside Peter in the forest clearing, he couldn't help a feeling of pride as the balloon — their third one — rose before his eyes.

The filled balloon strained against the lines that held it to the ground. The ropes wouldn't hold for long.

"Hurry!" Günter called.

The two families scrambled inside. Frank and Günter reached down to slice the lines. But only two ropes were cut right through. Under the strain, the third peg flew out of the ground.

The basket tipped over, held by one line. Everyone tumbled to the side. Peter struggled to control the burner — at this angle it was grazing the balloon. To his horror, flames ran up the fabric. Günter aimed the fire extinguisher and with a steady burst put them out.

Then he dropped the extinguisher and frantically hacked at the last line with his knife. The basket tipped back and began to rise. They sailed up into the darkness. Peter held the burner, while Günter kept an eye on the altimeter. Doris and Petra made sure the kids were safe.

They were moving fast in a cloudless sky filled with stars. Suddenly Günter's shout broke the silence. "Below! Spotlights!"

Beams of light from the border watchtowers swung across the sky, crisscrossing in midair. Peter frantically tried to remember — do they have anti-aircraft guns at the border? He didn't think so. He told himself that their machine guns couldn't fire this high.

He opened the burner valve. The flame streaked higher into the balloon, and they shot up above the lights.

Then, his heart sinking, Peter saw the flame sputter. Quickly he cranked open the valve as far as it could go. But he couldn't get a steady flame.

"How high are we?" he asked Günter.

"About 6,500 feet, but we're going down!"

The flame got smaller as Peter struggled with the burner. Then it dawned on him. We're out of fuel! How could that be? We've been flying for 23 minutes, he thought. We should have enough for 35 minutes. But there was no denying it. His calculations must have been wrong.

The flame flickered and went out. He could feel the balloon sinking. Below, they could see traffic lights. No, not yet, Peter thought wildly.

Günter grabbed the matches and tore out a handful. Striking them all at once, he held them to the burner. For a few seconds, a final flame streamed out.

The balloon soared upward briefly before the flame died. But was it enough?

Suddenly they were spinning, dropping, unable to steer. Peter strained to see through the darkness. Murky shapes were rushing toward them, getting larger as they fell earthward. Hills and trees, then farms.

They grabbed the posts and braced themselves for the crash. Branches brushed the basket's sides as they hurtled forward. Helpless, Peter clung to his post. Then he felt the earth beneath them.

The basket skimmed the grass, slowed, and came to a stop. Before they had caught their breath, it started to tip. Peter looked up — the balloon had caught in a tree and was dragging the basket over. He rushed to steady the propane bottles, while Günter cut the lines, freeing them of the balloon.

Everyone shook as they climbed out. They had flown for 28

minutes, thought Peter. Not long enough!

"Peter and I will look around," said Günter. "If it's safe, I'll light a flare. But if you don't see it, stay put!" Doris, Petra, and the kids hid in the trees as the two men walked away.

Across a field they spotted a large barn, its door hanging open. Peter and Günter ventured inside and swung the flashlight around.

The sound of a car pulling to a stop outside made them jump. Peter and Günter ducked behind the wall and peeked out. The car's headlights were aimed at the field. Peter could see two men in the front seats. Border police?

They must have tracked the balloon with the spotlights, then radar, thought Peter. They followed us straight to the crash site!

The two figures in the car got out and looked around.

Peter glanced desperately around for another way out of the barn. They're going to spot us any second, he thought.

Günter stared at the car — it was an Audi. Not what the cops usually drive, he thought. On its side, the single word "POLICE" shone in the dark. He'd never seen a police car like that before. Then suddenly it occurred to him.

That was no East German police car.

★ ★ ★

The police officers jumped when they saw two men running toward them from the barn. Wild-eyed, one of them was calling breathlessly, "Are we in West Germany?"

The policemen were so startled they just nodded. Shouts and hoots of joy pierced their ears. Before they had time to ask the strangers any questions, they were nearly knocked over as the two men hugged them.

"We made it!" the men shouted, jumping up and down. Then

one of them pulled a flare out of his pocket and lit it. The policemen looked at each other, mouths open. What was going on?

Now women and kids were running toward them across the field. Everyone was talking at once, but they managed to hear one thing clearly. These people claimed to have just landed in a hot-air balloon!

"Come on," the policemen chided. "Where did you people really come from?"

Petra led one of the officers to the site of the crash. But once there, she appeared to remember something. She reached inside the basket and drew out a carefully bundled package. Taking it back to the others, she unwrapped it while they watched.

"Champagne!" she cried, and they all laughed as she showed them the bottle. Petra had heard that every balloon flight needed a bottle of champagne for good luck.

★ ★ ★

It wasn't until four a.m. that the refugees popped the cork — in the town police station. Together they drank a toast to their amazing flight, and to the new life that lay ahead.

Reporters wanted to know why they had risked so much to escape to the West. Peter answered with the words he had carefully chosen to explain his actions. They wanted to live as free people, who could say what they thought and go where they wanted. And they wanted a good future for their children. The press called them heroes, but Peter disagreed.

"There's nothing heroic about wanting to be free," he said. "In any case, our desire for freedom far outweighed our fear."

Slaves of the Sahara

North Atlantic Coast of Africa, Off Cape Bajador, 1815

"TEN O'CLOCK!" CRIED THE MAN AT THE HELM. Through the fog, Captain Riley eyed the mainsail boom. It stretched far out to starboard, the ship running ahead of a strong breeze. The helmsman turned to port, and as the boom swung across the deck, Riley heard a roaring.

A squall? Startled, Riley glanced down the ship's lee side. Through a hole in the mist, he glimpsed rough water foaming below. Breakers!

"All hands on deck!" he shouted.

Working fast, the men dropped anchor and hauled in the sails. The ocean roared around them as they struggled to slow the ship before it hit the rocks. Waves swept across the deck, knocking the sailors off their feet.

For days, fog had made it hard to fix their position, but until now Riley had no idea how off-course they were. The *Commerce,* an American brig loaded with cargo, was headed from Gibraltar to the Canary Islands. Now its young captain knew the worst — they had been blown up against the North African coast, where deadly breakers pounded the rocky shoreline.

Riley's practical mind raced. The ship was beyond hope — pinned to the rocks and hammered by wave after wave. There was only one thing to do — save the crew before the vessel broke up and sank. The men worked quickly, knowing their lives depended on it. They grabbed all the water and provisions they could find, and threw overboard anything that would float. With luck some of it would wash ashore.

Riley fastened a sturdy rope to the ship's side. He signaled to his first mate, Porter, and the two men climbed down into the ship's small lifeboat, bringing the line with them. Waves broke over their bodies as they rowed desperately for the beach. A huge swell lifted their boat above the water, throwing them onto the sand. Riley scrambled for the line before it disappeared into the surf and tied it to a rock.

One by one the crew grasped the rope and lowered themselves out of the wreck, moving hand over hand along the line to shore. When the last exhausted sailor touched sand, they made a hasty camp on the beach. The ship's longboat washed ashore, its side smashed. Then came trunks of coins from their cargo. The men quickly buried the money in the sand.

Stopping to catch his breath, Riley scanned the sand dunes for other human beings. He wasn't in a hurry to see any. He knew that sailors shipwrecked on these shores were often captured and sold into slavery. Their best chance was to repair the leaky long-boat and try their luck out at sea. The men set to work, until darkness forced them to quit for the night.

At first light, Riley's fears were realized. Heads appeared over the dunes. Down the sandy hills sprinted a nimble gray-haired man, holding a spear. Younger men followed, armed with scimitars. Further off, Riley spotted more figures on camels approaching across the dunes. Soon they'd be surrounded!

Panicking, the sailors scrambled into the half-repaired long-boat and rowed frantically back to the *Commerce*. From the wreck,

Riley watched helplessly as the strangers plundered their camp. He gasped as one of them drove an axe into their casks, spilling the precious water onto the sand. Others dismounted from their camels and gathered the sea instruments and charts scattered across the beach. To Riley's horror, they burned them in a pile. Around him the crew clung to the wreck, tightening their grips with each sweeping wave that threatened to wash them off.

Then, to Riley's amazement, the men on the beach ran down to the water and put down their weapons at their feet. One of them held up a goatskin of water. Were they signaling peace?

The old man pointed to himself and then to the wreck. He wanted to come on board! He pointed to Riley and then to the beach. Riley understood: he was offering a trade — the captain for himself — to guarantee his safe return from the ship.

Riley quickly weighed their chances of getting out to sea through the pounding surf — slim indeed. They needed these people's help to survive. On a sudden impulse, he grabbed the line and worked his way back to the beach. The old man took Riley's place on the line and hauled himself toward the wreck. Once on board he looked around — for guns or money, Riley guessed.

Riley cupped his hands around his mouth and shouted to Porter: "Don't let him come back until they let me go!"

Porter put his hand to his ear and shook his head — he couldn't hear the captain over the roaring surf! Riley kept shouting, but his cries were lost in the din.

Finding nothing, the old man started back.

"Stop him!" Riley cried. He shot forward to the line. Strong hands grabbed his arms, as two men pulled him out of the water. Riley looked down at the scimitars they pointed at his chest, the metal blades glinting in the sun. He was their prisoner.

By now the old man had reached the sand, and the men started dragging Riley by the arms toward the dunes.

Riley thought fast. With frantic gestures, he signaled that a stash of coins was buried on the beach. The men stopped. One group headed for the spot he'd pointed out and began scraping at the sand. Two others sat Riley down with his face to the sea and pointed their scimitars at him — one to his chest, one to his head.

When they find the money, they'll probably shout, Riley thought. And my guards might look away for an instant. He'd have only one chance. Slowly, he drew his legs under him.

An excited shout was heard from behind. Riley's guards jerked their heads around. In a flash Riley sprung out from under their weapons and dove for the beach.

Riley knew he was running for his life. Sprinting to the water's edge, he felt his pursuers close on his heels. He plunged head-first into the waves and pushed his way underwater with desperate strokes. He didn't dare come up for a breath! Finally, his lungs bursting, Riley broke through the surface and gasped for air.

He stole a quick look around. The old man was close behind, up to his chin in the rough water. His arm was raised, his spear aimed at Riley. As he pulled back to let it fly, a huge surf rolled over both of them, hurtling the old man onto the beach.

Riley turned and swam furiously toward the wreck. Wave after wave broke over him. Each time he surfaced he glimpsed the crew on board, shouting and urging him on. At last he threw his arm up along the side, but a heavy surf pushed him down. Then he felt the grip of his mates' hands hauling him up.

Riley collapsed on the deck, exhausted. Over him stood Savage, the second mate, watching the beach. "What's happening?" Riley panted.

"Nothing — they're just staring out over the water. They can't believe you made it! Wait, now they're dragging our cargo toward the dunes." After a few moments, Savage shook his head. "I can't see them anymore... they're gone."

But they'll be back, thought Riley, pulling himself up. And there will be more of them. He gazed grimly at the rough sea. They wouldn't survive for long out there in the shattered longboat. But what else could they do? The wreck would soon smash to pieces. And the beach meant either slavery or death.

The longboat was their last chance. The crew threw in what little provisions were still on the wreck — a small keg of water, some salt pork, and a few figs. The eleven men took their places in the leaky hull, and two started bailing out water.

Riley put it to a vote. They could take their chances out at sea, or they could stick close to the rocky coast — and risk another wreck or attack. The men all agreed. They'd take the sea.

★ ★ ★

Riley's eyes were bleary from searching the horizon for a vessel. Six days at sea, and still nothing. Only the odd flash of lightning broke the gloomy haze. Under his feet the hastily patched boat creaked, and water seeped in constantly. He looked at the sunburned bodies of his crew, at the exhausted men who had to be prodded to keep bailing. His mouth was so parched that his orders came out in a hoarse whisper. How much longer would the water and pork hold out? As it was, their rations were barely giving them strength to row.

When the sun rose on the seventh day, Riley knew they couldn't go on. Then a shout broke through his grim thoughts.

"Land!"

Hope swept through the boat as the men turned in the direction of their mate's outstretched hand. Riley craned his neck — there it was! Far off, a perfectly smooth coast. No hill broke its straight line.

A desert, he realized, his heart sinking.

The men rowed for the coast. On shore Riley staggered from the boat and looked around. Jagged rocks loomed overhead, stretching as far as he could see in either direction. The men unloaded what was left of their water and salt pork and began to walk eastward along the coast — maybe they'd find a place to dig for water or get inland past the cliffs.

A fierce sun beat down on them. Hunger gnawed at Riley. He trudged onward, his eyes on the stony, red ground beneath him, baked hard by the sun. Spotting a few locusts, he grabbed them to stuff in his mouth, but they crumbled to dust at his touch.

I brought these men here, he thought. He stole a glance at young Horace, who was bravely keeping up with the bigger men. Riley had promised the cabin boy's mother that he would take care of him like a son.

After sunset, a crewman named Clark suddenly pointed ahead. "I see a light!" he cried.

A campfire! Hope thrilled through Riley. He saw the same feeling on the faces of his crew, but he raised an arm to hold them back. "Let's make camp for the night," he said. The men began to protest, but he shook his head. "Whoever they are, we don't want to alarm them by surprising them in the dark. Better to go in the morning."

The men wet their mouths with their last drops of water and settled down to sleep on the sand, which was still hot from the sun's rays. Riley lay awake, haunted by fears. They were unarmed, defenseless. Tomorrow they would probably be captured as slaves.

We must do what we can to stay alive, he told himself. Stay alive long enough to find a way, somehow, to get home.

★ ★ ★

Clambering over the dunes, Savage and Riley peered down into the valley nestled between sandy hills. Men and women milled around a well, fetching water for their camels — hundreds of them! Glancing up, a few men spotted the sailors and began to run toward them. At their sides, Riley could see the glint of steel in the sun — scimitars and muskets! Pulling Savage with him, he stepped forward.

The strangers wasted no time on words, and began to strip off the sailors' clothing. More people came running, and the air filled with shouts and excitement. Fights broke out over the windfall of new slaves.

The sailors were dragged away by their new masters, and women drove them toward the well with sticks. His shoes gone, Riley found it hard to walk barefoot over the hot sand, but each sharp whack from the stick sent him forward. Riley turned to the woman behind him and opened his parched mouth, pointing to it. She drew water from the well and began filling bowls.

The sailors fell upon the bowls of water. Slow down! Riley told himself. It was dangerous to drink so much at once when you have been dying of thirst. But he couldn't help himself. At last Riley raised his head from the bowl and, wiping his mouth, looked around.

The crowd was breaking up as each family moved off, its goatskins filled with water. We're going to be split up, Riley thought with horror. Porter and five other mates were already being led away on camels, their eyes wide and terrified. Riley had time only to grasp their hands as they passed. An instant later they slipped through a crevice in the cliff wall, and disappeared out of sight.

★ ★ ★

Riley clutched at the camel's hair, hanging on. His legs stretched painfully across the animal's broad back. Its backbone is as sharp as the edge of an oar's blade, thought Riley. Worst of all, the camel's sides, bloated with water, were perfectly smooth. Riley kept sliding down toward the camel's tail, then pulling himself back by its hair.

Frightened by the stranger on its back, the camel ran about, bellowing. Riley searched for a bridle or halter to guide it with — but found nothing. All he could do was hang on. Nearby, struggling in much the same way, were four of his shipmates — Savage, Clark, Horace, and Dick, the cook.

Up ahead their masters sat cross-legged on wooden saddles, their camels trotting across the flat landscape of sand and gravel. Women and children rode in huge baskets strapped to camels' backs.

The sun beat fiercely on Riley's bare skin and reflected off the sand, blinding him. Riley closed his eyes. His swaying camel felt like a small boat in a stormy sea.

Night came, and still there was no sign that the band of desert nomads would stop. The wind turned cold and cut through Riley's skin.

I can't take any more! he thought wildly. He looked down at the ground racing beneath him. If I fall off I could break my neck, he thought. But staying on was too painful. He let go and quickly slipped off the camel, tumbling to the ground. The group did not even pause. Riley scrambled on foot to keep up, the sharp stones cutting his unprotected feet.

At last the caravan stopped. The nomads milked the camels and gave the slaves a little to drink. Women quickly assembled tents for shelter from the cold night wind. Riley staggered toward a tent, but was beaten back with a stick. He and his crew were sent to lie down next to the camels. They collapsed onto the stony ground, where the desert wind swept over them unchecked.

Weeks passed in a blur of burning sun, swaying camels, and night winds. But Riley forced himself to stay sharp and listen to his masters' talk. It reminded him of Spanish — ancient Arabic, he guessed. He even learned a few words, and by watching their faces and hands, could catch the drift of their conversations.

That was how he discovered they were turning back to the well where he and his men had been captured. They couldn't survive any longer without water for the camels, whose milk was keeping them all alive.

Looking at the starved faces of his crew, Riley's heart sank. We're not going to make it there, he thought.

★ ★ ★

Riley panted in the shade of the tent — gratefully out of the midday sun. At his side lay Clark, barely conscious. Their masters had left early in the morning on their camels. The women had allowed the five slaves to rest near the tents in the meantime.

A month had passed since their capture, yet to Riley it seemed like years. He scanned the flat landscape that stretched in every direction. It's like the sea, he thought, like a smooth sea, when there's no wind. But the idea gave him no comfort.

His eyes grew heavy, but a movement on the horizon made him blink and open them wider. Two strangers on camels were approaching across the sand. As they came closer, Riley could see that their camels were loaded with goods and muskets that shone like silver in the sun. The riders stopped before the tent of Riley's master and, making their camels lie down, dismounted. Then they sat on the ground without a word, looking the other way.

The women of the family leapt up and began to rig an awning for the strangers. To Riley's surprise, his master's wife turned and approached him. Slowly, she spoke to him for the first time. Riley followed her words and gestures closely, piecing together her meaning.

"Sidi Hamet," she said, pointing to one of the strangers, "and his brother are cloth merchants from the Sultan's lands." She paused, then added in a low voice, "Perhaps he could buy you and take you there, where you might find your friends and kiss your wife and children." Then she walked away.

Riley's heart beat faster. He scanned the horizon again — no sign yet of his master. He snatched up a wooden bowl and ventured to the strangers' tent. Crouching down under their awning, Riley held up the bowl and showed his parched mouth to them. The man called Sidi Hamet asked him a question, and Riley recognized the word for "captain."

Riley nodded eagerly, "Yes, I am the captain."

Gathering heaps of sand in his hands, Riley made a coast on the ground. Then he drew the shape of a boat, adding a stick for a mast. With words and signs he prayed would capture the merchant's sympathy, Riley told the story of their shipwreck.

"I have a wife and five children back home... besides Horace, my son," he added, remembering his promise to the boy's mother. Hamet stared at him as he spoke, then turned his face away suddenly. Was he moved? How much had he understood? Riley wasn't sure.

Hamet motioned to his brother to give Riley some water, but the brother sullenly shook his head. Hamet signaled to Riley to hold up his bowl, and he poured it himself.

Clear, perfectly clear water streamed into the bowl. It was the first fresh water Riley had seen since they left the boat, and for a moment he was afraid he would faint. He drank half and then, gesturing toward Clark, asked to take the rest to him. Hamet nodded.

As Riley propped Clark up to drink, his shipmate's sunken eyes began to shine. Clark was mere skin and bones now, and Riley knew he would have to work fast.

The noise of approaching camels made Riley look up. Their masters were back. So soon! Riley felt sick with disappointment. His chance had slipped away — he did not dare approach the merchants again now. He'd have to watch for a chance to speak to them alone. In the meantime, his mind began to form a plan.

★ ★ ★

For days Riley shadowed the merchants as closely as he dared, terrified to take his eyes off them. They could be up and away at any moment.

Hamet feels sorry for us, he thought. I need to show him that helping us is worth his while! If he thinks there's money in it — a lot of money — he might buy us and carry us off the Sahara. If only I could get him alone! But Riley's master and his sons were never far away, and they glared ferociously at him whenever he lingered near the visitors.

Standing near the camels, Riley watched as his masters retreated from the afternoon heat into their tent. The two merchants moved back toward their own awning, Hamet trailing a little behind his brother.

This was his chance! Riley stumbled across the hot sand and fell to his knees before the merchant. With gestures and the few Arabic words he had practiced, he got his message across: "Carry me to the Sultan of Morocco, and my friend there will redeem me."

Riley's face fell as Hamet shook his head. The merchant stepped away, then paused.

"But," he said, turning back, "how much will you give me if I take you to Mogadore?" Riley had never heard of the place. With hand signs Hamet described it as a walled town and a seaport.

A seaport! Riley's heart raced. He made a pile of fifty stones. "That many dollars for myself and each of my men," he said, pointing.

Again, Hamet shook his head, waving his arm in the direction of the crew. "Not the others," he said. He jabbed a finger at the stones, then at Riley. "But how much more than that will you give me, if I buy *you*?"

Riley frantically counted out fifty more stones and added them to the first pile. "My friend will pay you as soon as you bring me to Mogadore," he said. His heart pounded as he watched Hamet's stony expression.

A moment passed in silence. At last Hamet nodded, pointing to Riley. "I will buy *you* then," he said. "But remember, if you deceive me..." He made a cutting motion across his throat.

Riley swallowed and nodded.

"Say nothing to your master," Hamet added as he turned to leave, "nor to my brother."

In the days that followed, Riley shadowed Hamet, begging him to buy just one more of the men — perhaps his son, Horace? "The ransom for all of us together would be even more," he promised.

But Hamet shook his head. "Impossible to get you all across the desert — robbers will attack us for our slaves, and my brother and I cannot fight them off."

Then Hamet pointed at Clark's wasted body. "He will not live more than three days. If I buy him, I'll lose my money!"

"I swear I will pay for him," said Riley, lowering his voice, "whether he lives or dies."

★ ★ ★

The merchants inspected the sailors from head to toe — parting their hair with sticks, frowning at their burned skin and blisters. They prodded their bones to see if they were in place.

Hamet's brother stood back and shook his head in disgust. "You will make a big mistake, my brother, to buy any more of them."

But one evening Hamet told Riley they would all leave at dawn. "I have used up all my goods buying the whole crew. My brother tried to talk me out of it," Hamet said. "He doesn't believe you have any rich friend who will pay for you." Riley looked down.

"You had better not deceive me," Hamet added, his tone menacing.

At first light they set off across the blowing sand. Savage muttered at Riley's side, voicing all the doubts Riley had ignored until now. "How do we know they're taking us where they say? And how on earth do you expect to pay them? There might not be an English consul — or any consul at all — at this seaport."

Riley stared ahead.

"And if there is," Savage went on, "you've promised too much! Who's going to lend you that much money? We're poor sailors, not rich men. Who pays a ransom for a poor man?" Riley was silent. Everything Savage said was true. He was taking a desperate gamble. And he remembered the penalty if he couldn't pay — his life.

The five sailors stumbled forward under the fierce sun. Like sleepwalkers they followed the merchants' swaying camels across endless stretches of sand. Riley had no idea how his wasted legs were able to keep moving, unless it was the new hope — a very slim one — that lay on the other side of the Sahara.

★ ★ ★

It took a moment for Riley's groggy mind to recognize the signs. Beneath his stumbling feet he saw something green. Something ragged and parched, but growing. Plants — they were near the edge of the desert! Then came the sound of distant voices, and small huts on the horizon.

As they made camp that night, Hamet took Riley aside. "I will set out in the morning for Mogadore," he said, "where I hope to arrive in three days. If your friend will pay the money for you and your men, you shall be free."

He stared hard at Riley. "If not, you must die for having deceived me, and your men shall be sold for what they will bring. I have suffered hunger and thirst to restore you to your family, for I believe God is with you. I have paid away all my money on your word alone."

"Take me with you," Riley begged. Hamet shook his head.

"My brother will guard you while I'm gone," he said firmly.

Riley looked down, but his new master beckoned to him. "Come, Riley. Write a letter." He held out a scrap of paper, smaller than Riley's hand. Riley took it, and Hamet gave him a little bit of black liquid and a reed.

Riley dipped the reed in the ink and held it for a moment over the shred of paper. All at once he saw how truly hopeless his scheme was. He had no "friend" in Mogadore, no idea if there was any consul there. Who would read his note? And if anyone did, why would they hand over so much money because of a scrap of paper from a stranger — a slave?

He glanced up and saw Sidi Hamet watching him. Taking a deep breath, he carefully began to write.

Sir,

The brig Commerce *was wrecked on the 28 of August last. Myself and four of my crew are here nearly naked in slavery. I conjure you by all the ties that bind man to man... and by as much as liberty is dearer than life, to advance the money required for our redemption, which is nine hundred and twenty dollars. I can draw for any amount the moment I am at liberty...*

Should you not relieve me, my life must instantly pay the forfeit.

Worn down to the bones — naked and a slave, I implore your pity...

James Riley, late Master of the brig Commerce

Riley folded the paper and paused. Who would he send it to? He dipped the reed in the little liquid that remained and scratched desperately,

To the English, French, Spanish or American consul, or any merchant in Mogadore

He silently handed the paper to Sidi Hamet and watched his master turn and walk away. He had done all he could. Now his life was in someone else's hands.

★ ★ ★

Riley sat with his shipmates, watching the sun disappear behind the small huts that dotted the horizon. That makes it eight days since Hamet left for Mogadore, Riley thought grimly. Still they had heard nothing. He lay awake at nights, his mind swinging feverishly between hope and fear. He pictured Hamet searching in vain for someone who would read his letter — never mind pay the money! He must be angry by now, thought Riley. He must think I tricked him.

The sound of anyone coming — an opening gate, the trample of hooves — made Riley jump. He couldn't wait for his master to return, and at the same time he dreaded it. It would be the moment that either set him free, or ended his life.

A voice from nowhere made Riley and his men leap to their feet. "How de-do Cap-e-tan."

English! Riley couldn't remember the last time anyone but his crew had spoken to him in his own language. A man was walking toward them. Speaking in a mixture of English and Spanish, he explained that an Englishman had sent him from Mogadore. He handed Riley a letter.

Riley's heart was in his mouth as he took it. His shipmates stared at the letter with wide eyes, knowing it spelled out their fate. With shaking hands, Riley unfolded the paper and began to read.

My dear and afflicted sir,
    I have this moment received your note…

Riley's eyes scanned down the page to the only words that mattered.

I have agreed to pay the sum of nine hundred and twenty dollars to Sidi Hamet on your safe arrival in this town with your fellow sufferers. He remains here as a kind of hostage for your safe appearance…
    … with the hope of a happy end to all your sufferings, I subscribe myself, my dear Sir,

                        Your friend,
                        William Willshire

Riley stared for a moment at the name he'd never heard before. The name of a stranger. A stranger who had saved him. Joy and wonder began to swell inside him. He raised a hand to his gaunt face, and felt that his cheeks were wet with tears.

★ ★ ★

When Captain Riley returned home to the United States he wrote a book about his adventures. Riley's *Narrative* was read by over a million people, including a young boy named Abraham Lincoln. Some historians suggest that two events helped set the future American president's mind against slavery. One was his visit to a slave market in New Orleans when he was 19. And the other, earlier experience may have been reading Captain Riley's tale of slavery and escape.

Tickets to Freedom

Macon, Georgia, 1848

THERE WERE ONLY A FEW DAYS LEFT before Christmas, as a young black slave named William Craft hurried home through the dusk to the cottage he shared with his wife, Ellen. In the pocket of his coat he felt the pair of dark eyeglasses he'd bought moments before. Slaves weren't supposed to buy such things without their master's permission, but some storekeepers were ready to take a slave's money and not ask too many questions.

For weeks now, William had been buying pieces of clothing one at a time — a shirt here, a hat there, all at different stores so as not to attract too much attention. The green glasses were the finishing touch on a plan, a bold and dangerous scheme William and Ellen had worked out together: their bid for freedom.

★ ★ ★

William and Ellen had always known they were luckier than many slaves. Ellen worked in her mistress' house as a lady's maid. William's master had paid to train him as a carpenter and then hired him out, taking most of William's pay but letting him keep a little for himself. Life was better for them than for the slaves on a cotton plantation — theirs was hard, back-breaking work, never far from an overseer's watchful eye and sharp whip.

Still, they had longed for freedom. William was tired of working hard only to hand over his wages to someone else. And Ellen could never shake the fear that all they had could be snatched away. If either of their masters needed money, she or William could be sold and they would never see each other again. Worst of all, any children they might have could be taken from them. William had watched helplessly while his parents were sold at an auction to the highest bidder — and he felt the same anger and sadness whenever he remembered. Ellen had been taken from her mother when she was 11, and now she couldn't bear the thought of raising a child to be someone's slave. At first they had put off getting married, hoping to escape and marry once they were free.

Other slaves had done it. They'd followed the Underground Railroad — which wasn't a railroad at all, but a long line of hiding places and secret helpers that ran from the southern slave states through the free north, all the way to Canada. Some slaves had even made a desperate run for it, following the North Star at night, hiding in woods and swamps during the day. With luck, they stumbled upon a friendly person who could tell them the way to the next safe house, or "station" along the railroad.

But Ellen and William wanted to come up with a plan before they made their move. Whenever they were alone they whispered together about all kinds of schemes, yet every one had its problems.

"A train or boat would get us out of Georgia the quickest. We could save for the fare," Ellen ventured.

William shook his head. "Not without permission from our masters. We can't even walk the roads without that. Any white person could stop us and ask for our passes, to show we had a right to be there. And then what?" He paused and added, "They'd send slave catchers after us, that's what."

Ellen was silent. They both knew about professional slave hunters. The way they tracked down runaways — on horseback with guns and dogs — reminded William of a fox hunt. He shuddered as he imagined himself and Ellen being dragged back to slavery. And not to their old jobs, either. They'd be punished as a lesson to other slaves — separated and sold "down the river" to a much harder life on a plantation.

The more they talked, the more impossible it seemed to make it across the slave states to freedom — a journey of nearly a thousand miles. Ellen and William asked for their masters' permission to marry, and they tried to make the best of it. But they never forgot their dream, and kept their eyes open for the smallest hope of escape.

★ ★ ★

Mending a drawer in his workshop one December afternoon, William puzzled over the problems that stood in their way. Slaves couldn't get on a train or boat without permission. As he sanded, he pictured Ellen. She was so fair-skinned; she had a white father, after all. A bold plan began to form in William's mind. What if Ellen pretended to be white, while William traveled as her slave?

But no, he knew a southern lady would never travel alone with a male servant. Then a sudden idea made his hand pause on the wood. Ellen could disguise herself as a white *man*. They could escape in daylight, under the noses of the slaveholders themselves! They'd travel first-class to Philadelphia — in the free state of Pennsylvania — and from there through the northern states to Canada.

It was risky, he thought, but so unexpected that it might have a chance. He knew that some slaveholders gave their favorite slaves a few days' holiday around Christmas. If he and Ellen could get time off, it would give them a head start before they were missed.

That night William described his plan to Ellen. She was too shocked to speak at first. How could she keep up a disguise like that for hundreds of miles across the slave states? No, thought Ellen, it was too crazy. Then she pictured the life that lay before her if she did nothing — years of work without anything to call their own, not even their own bodies. And always the fear of losing her husband, her future children to the auction block. She looked at William and nodded — she would take the risk.

William began to buy as many pieces of her disguise as he could, a little at a time. Ellen was extra careful to please her mistress before she asked for a pass to be away for a few days, and the cabinetmaker gave William a pass without too much fuss. They hurried home to show each other their passes, but neither could read them — it was illegal to teach slaves to read. They'd have to trust that the passes said what they hoped.

So far all the pieces were falling into place. But as the day of escape drew closer, Ellen began to notice flaws in their plan. "William, any traveling gentleman would sign his name to register at a hotel — and I can't write!"

William slumped in his chair — he hadn't thought of that. Ellen paced the cottage floor anxiously. Then her face lit up. "I think I have it — I'll bind up my right hand in a sling, and ask the innkeeper to sign for me."

Then, glimpsing herself in a mirror, she frowned — her face was too smooth to convince anyone that she was a man! She pulled some cloth out of her sewing box and wound it into a bundle. Wrapping it around her chin with a handkerchief, she tied the ends over her head.

"As if I had a bad toothache," she explained, turning to show

William. He agreed it could work. And it would give her an excuse to avoid chatting with other travelers — the less she had to talk, the better.

Four more nights passed as they stayed up late, talking over their plan in the darkness. The sling and handkerchief gave William more ideas. If Ellen acted sick and lost in her thoughts, people wouldn't bother her. Like many slave owners, she'd count on her slave to fetch and carry for her — and answer questions from any nosy fellow travelers. And in only a few days, they could be free!

★ ★ ★

The moment they had so eagerly awaited was almost at hand. Ellen's costume was nearly finished. Whatever William hadn't been able to buy, Ellen had sewn herself in her moments alone. The evening before their escape, William brought home the pair of glasses that would complete the picture. The dark lenses would hide any fear in Ellen's eyes. They both knew she would have to sit surrounded by white men — and slave owners — wherever they traveled.

Just before dawn, William cut off Ellen's long hair. With trembling hands she slipped on her dark suit, cloak, and hat, then the high-heeled boots that would make her look taller. As she stood leaning on a cane, with one arm in a sling and bandages on her face, William took a long look at her. He smiled and shook his head in disbelief — she looked so much like a sickly white gentleman he was almost convinced himself!

It was time to go. They blew out the candles, and a sudden noise made them jump — was someone outside? Holding hands, they peeked out the cottage door. Everything was still. Silently they tiptoed outside and stood breathless, looking at each other.

From now on they would be traveling apart most of the time—blacks did not sit next to whites on trains and in boats. Without speaking they clasped hands, and then left in different directions for the rail station. William headed for the railcar reserved for blacks, and Ellen, leaning on her cane, limped to the first-class carriage. In her new identity as a young planter called Mr. Johnson, she bought a ticket for herself and one slave for Savannah — their first stop. There was no going back now.

Inside the carriage, Ellen took a window seat and stared outside. Sit still, she told herself. Don't attract attention. As the train slowly chugged away from the station, she glanced around the carriage — and froze. Mr. Cray, an old friend of her master who had known her since she was a child, had sat next to her while she was looking the other way. Ellen fought the urge to bolt, and turned slowly back toward the window. Why had he said nothing? Maybe he hadn't recognized her yet. If he strikes up a conversation, thought Ellen, he'll be sure to know my voice. Desperate, she decided to pretend to be deaf.

Mr. Cray soon turned to her and said politely, "It is a very fine morning, sir."

Ellen kept staring out the window. Mr. Cray repeated his greeting, but Ellen did not move. A passenger nearby laughed. Annoyed, Mr. Cray said, "I will make him hear," then, very loudly, "IT IS A VERY FINE MORNING, SIR."

Ellen turned her head as if she had only just heard him, bowed politely and said, "Yes." Then she turned back to the window.

"It is a great hardship to be deaf," another passenger remarked.

Mr. Cray nodded. "I will not trouble the gentleman anymore."

Ellen began to breathe more easily — he hadn't recognized her! Her disguise had passed a difficult test, but she realized more than ever how wary she must be.

The train pulled into Savannah early in the evening. William was waiting for Ellen outside her carriage, and they headed next for a steamboat bound for Charleston. Once on board, Ellen slipped into her room and shut the door. What a relief to be alone! But some of the passengers grumbled to William that this was strange. Why wasn't his young master staying up and being friendly?

William hurried to Ellen's room and told her about the reaction. They couldn't afford to do anything suspicious. But she couldn't very well play cards and smoke cigars without giving herself away! Ellen thought quickly: William could go heat up the bundle of medicine for her face on the stove in the gentlemen's saloon, to make it look as if his master was ill and going to bed early. The men in the saloon complained loudly about the smell the hot herbs made and sent William away. But they seemed convinced that his master must be pretty sick!

Once Ellen had turned in, William went on deck and asked the steward where he could sleep. The steward shook his head — no beds for black passengers, slave or free. William's heart sank, but he said nothing. As expected, his journey was turning out to be very different from Ellen's! Weary, he paced the deck for a while, then found some cotton bags in a warm spot near the smokestack and sat there until morning.

At breakfast, the ship's captain invited Ellen to sit at his table, and he asked politely about her health. William stood nearby to cut Ellen's food, since her arm was in a sling. When he stepped out for a moment, the captain gave Ellen some friendly advice: "You have a very attentive boy, sir; but you had better watch him like a hawk when you get on to the North."

A slave dealer sitting nearby agreed that William would probably make a run for it, and offered to buy him then and there. "No," Ellen answered carefully. "I cannot get on well without him."

Later up on deck a young southern officer warned Ellen that she would spoil her slave by saying "thank you" to him. "The only way to keep him in his place," he declared, "is to storm at him like thunder, and keep him trembling like a leaf."

I feel sorry for his slaves, thought Ellen. But from then on she remembered not to be so nice to William in front of people.

By now the boat had reached the wharf at Charleston, but when Ellen saw the crowd waiting for the steamer she shrank back. All those people — someone might recognize William. Or what if their owners already knew they had escaped and had sent someone to arrest them? She led William back to her cabin, where they waited nervously until every other passenger had left. At the last minute they stepped onto the empty wharf, and William ordered a carriage to take them to the best hotel.

When the innkeeper saw Ellen in her fine clothes and sling he pushed William aside and showed Ellen to one of the best rooms. Ellen would have loved to rest, but she knew the curious servants were expecting her downstairs for dinner. While she was led to the elegant dining room, William was handed a plate of food and sent to the kitchen to eat. Looking down, he saw that the plate was broken and that his knife and fork were rusty. William sighed but wasn't much surprised. He ate quickly and returned to wait on his "master," not wanting to leave Ellen alone for too long. As he entered the dining room he tried not to smile — three servants were already fussing over Ellen, each hoping for a tip from such a fine gentleman.

★ ★ ★

Ellen and William had planned to take a steamboat from Charleston to Philadelphia — and freedom! But at the inn Ellen learned that the steamer didn't run during winter. Their only choice now was the Overland Mail Route. They could take a steamer to Wilmington, North Carolina, and catch the mail train there. Ellen tried to hide her disappointment. This was a longer route — and the longer their journey, the more chances of being caught.

There was no choice but to press on. The next day, William and Ellen headed for the crowded ticket office, where Ellen asked for two tickets to Philadelphia. The mean-looking man behind the counter looked up and stared at William suspiciously. Then he asked Ellen to register her name and the name of her slave in his book.

Ellen ignored his glare. She pointed to the sling on her arm. "Would you kindly sign for me, please?" The man shook his head and stubbornly stuck his hands in his pockets. William glanced around and saw that people had stopped to stare at them. The last thing they wanted was more attention.

Stay calm, Ellen told herself, and she was thankful for the dark glasses that hid her eyes.

She was about to speak again when she heard a voice call "Mr. Johnson!" Ellen spun around. The young officer she had met on the last steamer — the one who had told her not to be so polite to her slave — was pushing through the crowd. He patted her on the back and cheerfully told the ticket seller, "I know his kin like a book."

At this the captain of the Wilmington steamboat, who had been watching silently nearby, spoke up. "I'll register the gentleman's name," he declared, no doubt realizing that he was about to lose a passenger, "and take the responsibility upon myself."

Once the steamer was on its way, the captain took Ellen aside to explain. They were always very strict at Charleston — you never knew when a sympathetic white person might try to help a slave run away by pretending to be his master.

"I suppose so," Ellen said casually.

The next day they switched to a train for Baltimore. Once again, William rode in a separate car while Ellen sat in a first-class carriage, this time with a gentleman from Virginia and his two daughters.

"What seems to be the matter with you, sir?" the man asked her in a kindly tone.

"Rheumatism," Ellen replied. He nodded and insisted that Ellen lie down.

Good idea, thought Ellen, the less chatting the better. The daughters made a pillow for her with their shawls and covered her with a cloak. While Ellen pretended to sleep, she heard one of them sigh and whisper, "Papa, he seems to be a very nice young gentleman." Her sister added, "I never felt so much for a gentleman in my life!" When Ellen told William about it he laughed. They had certainly fallen in love with the wrong man!

Before leaving the train, the girls' father handed Ellen a recipe — his "sure cure" for rheumatism. Ellen didn't dare pretend to read it. What if she held it the wrong way? So she thanked him and tucked it in her pocket.

★ ★ ★

It was Christmas Eve as the train slowed to its stop at Baltimore, where they would switch to a train for Philadelphia. This was the last "slave port" on their journey, and Ellen felt more nervous than ever. We're so close now, she told herself. Only one more night to get through. She and William knew that people kept a keen eye out for runaways in Baltimore, to stop them from escaping into the free state of Pennsylvania. They could lose everything just in sight of their goal.

As usual, William helped Ellen into the first-class carriage when they switched trains. He was about to board his own car when he felt a tap on his shoulder. He turned to face an officer, who asked sharply, "Where are you going, boy?"

"To Philadelphia, sir," William answered humbly, "with my master — he's in the next carriage."

"Well, you had better get him, and be quick about it, because the train will soon be starting. It is against the rules to let any man take a slave past here, unless he can prove that he has a right to take him along." He then brushed past William and moved down the platform.

William stood frozen for a moment, not knowing what to

do. Then he stepped into the first-class carriage and saw Ellen sitting alone. She looked up at him and smiled. He knew what she was thinking: they would be free by dawn the next morning. William struggled to keep his voice steady as he told her the bad news. Ellen's face fell. To be caught this close to freedom! She looked searchingly at William, but he was speechless. What choice did they have? Run for it now? They would be caught before they were outside the station. There was only one way — they would have to brave it out to the end.

Ellen led William to the station office and asked for the person in charge. A uniformed man stepped forward. Ellen felt his sharp eyes upon her.

"Do you wish to see me, sir?" she asked. The officer told her no one could take a slave to Philadelphia unless he could prove he was the rightful owner.

"Why is that?" Ellen demanded. The firmness in her voice surprised William. The officer explained that if someone posing as a slave owner passed through with a runaway, the real master could demand to be paid for his property.

This exchange began to attract the attention of other passengers. A few shook their heads and someone said that this was no way to treat an invalid gentleman. The officer, seeing that Ellen had the crowd's sympathy, offered a compromise.

"Is there any gentleman in Baltimore who could be brought here to vouch for you?"

"No," said Ellen. "I bought tickets in Charleston to pass us through to Philadelphia, and therefore you have no right to detain us here."

"Well, sir, right or no right, we shan't let you go," was the cold reply.

A few moments of silence followed. Ellen and William looked

at each other but were afraid to speak, in case they made a mistake that would show who they really were. They knew the officers could throw them in jail, and then it would only be a matter of time before their real identities were discovered and they were driven back to slavery. A wrong word now would be fatal.

Just then the conductor of the train they had left stepped in. He commented that they had indeed come on his train, and he left the room. The bell rang to signal their train's departure, and the sudden noise made everyone jump — all eyes fixed more keenly on them. Soon it would be too late.

The officer ran his fingers through his hair, and finally said, "I really don't know what to do; I calculate it is all right." He let them pass, grumbling, "As he is not well, it is a pity to stop him here."

Ellen thanked him and hobbled as quickly as she could with her cane toward her carriage. William leapt into his own railcar just as the train was leaving the platform.

Before long the train pulled to a halt alongside a river, where a ferry boat would carry the passengers to a train on the other side. When a porter asked Ellen to leave her seat and head for the ferry, she stood up and looked around for William. He always appeared as soon as the train stopped to "assist" her. Now he was nowhere in sight. On the platform she asked the conductor if he had seen her slave.

"No, sir," he said. "I haven't seen anything of him for some time." He added slyly, "I have no doubt he has run away, and is in Philadelphia, free, long before now."

Her panic rising, Ellen asked if he would look for William. "I am not a slave hunter," he huffed, and left her.

It was cold, dark, and raining as Ellen stood alone. Her mind started racing with possibilities — had William been left behind in Baltimore... or been kidnapped by slave catchers? Then with horror she remembered — she had no money. They had left it all with William because pickpockets wouldn't bother stealing from a slave. She looked down at the tickets in her hand, their tickets to freedom. They seemed worthless now that she had lost William.

Her time was up — everyone else had boarded the ferry. There's no going back, she thought. All she could do was press on to Philadelphia, and hope that someday she would find him.

★ ★ ★

William was closer than Ellen thought. They had been traveling day and night and sleeping very little. Fear and excitement had kept them awake until now. But finally, within hours of Philadelphia, William had nodded off. Sound asleep, he was tumbled out with the luggage onto a baggage boat.

A guard later found William and shook him awake. "Your master is scared half to death about you," he said.

William sat up, frightened — had something happened to Ellen? "Why?" he gasped.

"He thinks you have run away from him," the guard replied.

Relieved, William hurried to Ellen to let her know what had happened. The conductor and the guard laughed as if it were all a great joke. Then the guard took William aside and told him he really should run away once they got to Philadelphia.

"No, sir," William replied. "I shall never run away from such a good master." The guard was stunned, but William wasn't going to let anyone in on their secret — not yet.

Back in his own railcar, another passenger quietly told William of a boarding house in Philadelphia where he would be safe if he ran away. A station on the Underground Railroad! William thanked him, but did not say any more.

Just before dawn, William stuck his head out the train window. He could see flickering lights ahead in the distance. Then he heard a passenger say to his friend, "Wake up... we are at Philadelphia!" William felt as if a heavy burden had slipped off his back. He stared at the glittering city as the train sped on, and the sight made him lightheaded.

It was Christmas Day. Before the train had fully stopped, William was already running to Ellen's carriage. They hurried into a cab and William gave the driver the address of the boarding house he had heard about.

"Thank God, William, we are safe!" Ellen exclaimed, and broke into sobs. After pretending for so long, she felt drained. She leaned heavily on William as they stepped out of the cab and climbed the stairs to their room.

Ellen rested a while, then took off her disguise and changed into the women's clothing she had packed. She and William walked into the sitting room and asked to see the landlord. The man was confused. What happened to the young cotton planter he had seen arrive?

"But where is your master?" he asked William. William pointed to Ellen. "I'm not joking," the landlord replied, becoming annoyed.

It took some time to convince him of who they were! In the end, the innkeeper sent for some antislavery friends who could help them decide what to do next. William and Ellen had planned to go to Canada, following the Underground Railroad further north. But their new friends warned them that December in Canada would be much colder than they were used to in Georgia. They would face a hard first winter in an unfamiliar place.

But staying in Philadelphia wouldn't be safe either — slave catchers sometimes kidnapped runaways there, even though it was in a free state. Boston might be a better choice. Most people there were so against slavery that slave hunters didn't dare try. And so it was decided. Ellen and William stayed with a Quaker family until they were ready to leave for Boston, and a new life.

★ ★ ★

Even in Boston, the Crafts did not feel safe for long, however. Two years later, the Fugitive Slave Bill was passed. Slave catchers could now legally follow runaways into the free states and bring them back. With the help of Underground Railroad workers, Ellen and William escaped a warrant for their arrest and fled to Halifax, where they boarded a ship for England.

Abbott, G. *Great Escapes from the Tower of London*. London: Heinemann, 1982.

The Acts of Stephen, Roger of Wendover's Flowers of History. Excerpted in *Escape: An Anthology*. Edited by Michael Mason. London: Chatto & Windus, 1996.

The Anglo-Saxon Chronicle and *The Peterborough Chronicle*. The Online Medieval and Classical Library, University of California, Berkeley (sunsite.berkeley.edu/OMACL/Anglo).

Appleby, John T. *The Troubled Reign of King Stephen*. New York: Barnes & Noble Inc., 1970.

Bader, Douglas. *Fight for the Sky: The Story of the Spitfire and the Hurricane*. London: Sidgwick and Jackson, 1973.

Bradley, Keith R. *Slavery and Rebellion in the Roman World: 140 B.C.– 70 B.C.* Bloomington, Indiana: Indiana University Press, 1989.

Brickhill, Paul. *Reach for the Sky: The Story of Douglas Bader*. London: Collins, 1954, 1967.

Chamberlin, Russell. *The Tower of London: An Illustrated History.* London: Webb & Bower Ltd., 1989.

Chancellor, Henry. *Colditz: The Definitive History.* London: Hodder and Stoughton, 2001.

Craft, William. "Running a Thousand Miles to Freedom." In *Great Slave Narratives: Selected and Introduced by Arna Bontemps.* Boston: Beacon Press, 1969.

Eggers, Reinhold. *Colditz: The German Story.* Translated and edited by Howard Gee. London: Robert Hale Ltd., 1961 (Charnwood Edition 1999).

Foot, M. R. D. and J. M. Langley. *MI9: Escape and Evasion 1939–1945.* London: Bodley Head, 1979.

Hilton, Christopher. *The Wall: The People's Story.* Phoenix Mill, Great Britain: Sutton Publishing Ltd., 2001.

Jackson, Robert. *Douglas Bader: A Biography.* London: Arthur Barker Ltd., 1983.

Kiger, Patrick. "The Escape Psyche." From the Learning Channel/Discovery website (www. tlc.discovery.com/convergence/escape/articles/psyche.html)

Larive, E.H. *The Man Who Came in from Colditz.* London: Robert Hale Ltd., 1975.

"A Letter from the Countess of Nithsdale, 1827 (describing events of 1716)." In *Escape: An Anthology,* edited by Michael Mason. London: Chatto & Windus, 1996.

Lucas, Laddie. *Flying Colours: The Epic Story of Douglas Bader.* London: Hutchinson & Co., 1982.

McFadden, Robert D., Joseph B. Treaster and Maurice Carroll. *No Hiding Place: The New York Times Inside Report on the Hostage Crisis.* New York: Times Books, 1981.

Mears, Kenneth J. *The Tower of London: 900 Years of English History.* Oxford: Phaidon Press, 1988.

"Memoirs of Henry Masers de Latude, during a Confinement of Thirty-five Years in the State Prisons of France." English translation, 1787. Excerpted in *Escape: An Anthology.* Edited by Michael Mason. London: Chatto & Windus, 1996.

Memoirs of the Bastille by Latude and Linguet. (Including "Despotism Unmasked," a memoir by Jean Henri Masers de Latude) Translated by J. and S.F. Mills Whitman. London: George Routledge & Sons Ltd., 1927.

Ortzen, Len. *Stories of Famous Shipwrecks.* London: Arthur Barker Ltd., 1974.

Pelletier, Jean and Claude Adams. *The Canadian Caper.* Toronto: Macmillan, 1981.

Petschull, Jürgen. *With the Wind to the West: The Great Balloon Escape.* Translated by Courtney Searls. London: Hodder and Stoughton, 1981.

Prestwich, Michael. *Armies and Warfare in the Middle Ages.* New Haven: Yale University Press, 1996.

Quétel, Claude. *Escape from the Bastille: The Life and Legend of Latude.* Translated by Christopher Sharp. Cambridge: Polity Press, 1990.

Reid, P.R. *Colditz: The Full Story.* London: Macmillan, 1984.

Riley, James. *Sufferings in Africa: Captain Riley's Narrative.* (First published 1817) New York: Clarkson Potter, 2000.

Shaw, Brent D., ed. and trans. *Spartacus and the Slave Wars: A Brief History with Documents.* New York: Bedford/St. Martin's, 2001.

Still, William (Secretary of Pennsylvania Anti-slavery Society's General Vigilance Committee). *The Underground Railroad: A Record.* Chicago: Johnson Publishing Company Inc., 1970 (first published 1871).

Warner, Philip. *The Medieval Castle: Life in a Fortress in Peace and War.* London: Arthur Barker Ltd., 1972.

William of Malmesbury's *Historia Novella,* in *Contemporary Chronicles of the Middle Ages* translated by Joseph Stephenson (1850, repr. 1988). Excerpted on California State University Northridge website (www.csun.edu).

Index

About the Author

GROWING UP, Laura Scandiffio loved to read and write stories, draw pictures, put on plays with friends, and explore the woods and water near her home and cottage.

She has always been fascinated by stories of escape and survival, whether from real-life or in fiction. She enjoys traveling and the adventure of encountering different places, languages, and people.

Besides writing, Laura has worked as an editor of books for both children and adults. She is the author of *The Martial Arts Book,* also published by Annick Press. Laura lives in Toronto with her husband and two children.